Writing across the curriculum

Year 6

Maria Roberts

Maria Roberts teaches part time at West Hoathly Church of England Primary School in West Sussex. She has responsibility for able pupils.

Maria obtained a first class honours degree, lectured in literacy and began a PhD before deciding to spend more time with her family of three children.

Contents

Published by
Hopscotch Educational Publishing Ltd
Unit 2
The Old Brushworks
56 Pickwick Road
Corsham
Wiltshire
SN13 9BX

01249 701701

© 2004 Hopscotch Educational Publishing

Written by Maria Roberts
Series design by Blade Communications
Cover illustration by Susan Hutchison
Illustrated by Tony Randall
Printed by Colorman (Ireland) Ltd

ISBN 1-904307-37-X

Maria Roberts hereby asserts her moral right to be identified as
the author of this work in accordance with the Copyright, Designs
and Patents Act, 1988.

*The author and publishers would like to express their
gratitude to Rev Carr, Amy Radcliffe and West Hoathly
C of E Primary School.*

Introduction

About the series

Writing Across the Curriculum is a series of books aimed at developing and enriching the writing skills of children at Key Stage 2. Matched to the National Literacy Strategy's *Framework for Teaching* and the QCA's Schemes of Work, each book contains comprehensive lesson plans in two different subject areas for recount, report, instruction, explanation, persuasion and discussion (in Year 6) writing.

There are four books in the series: Year 3, Year 4, Year 5 and Year 6.

Each book aims to:

- support teachers by providing detailed lesson plans on how to incorporate the teaching of writing skills within different subject areas;
- develop teachers' confidence in using shared writing sessions by providing example scripts that the teachers can use or adapt;
- reduce teachers' preparation time through the provision of photocopiable resources;
- develop and enhance children's writing skills through stimulating and purposeful activities;
- encourage children's enjoyment of writing.

About each book

Each book is divided up into separate chapters for each writing genre. Each chapter contains:

- an introductory page of teacher's notes that outlines the key structural and linguistic features and guidelines on the teaching and progression of that particular writing genre;
- two units of work on a different subject area each.

Each unit of work is divided into four lesson plans that can be carried out over a period of time. These lessons are called:

- 'Switching on' – introduces the concepts;
- 'Revving up' – develops the concepts;
- 'Taking off' – instigates the planning stage of the writing;
- 'Flying solo' – encourages independent writing.

Each lesson plan is divided up as follows:

    Learning objectives;
    Resources required;
    What to do;
    Plenary.

Most lessons are supported by **photocopiable sheets**. Some of these sheets provide background information for the children and others provide support in the form of writing frames. Most lessons have an exemplar text that can be shared with the children. There is usually an annotated version of this text for the teacher. The annotated version points out the structural and linguistic features of the text. It should be noted, however, that only one example of each feature is provided and that the features are presented as a guide only.

Chapter 1

Recount writing

What is a recount text?

A recount is quite simply a retelling of an event. The retelling can be used to impart information or to entertain the reader. Recounts can be personal (from the point of view of someone who was there) or impersonal.

Structural features

- Usually begins with an introduction to orientate the reader. Often answers the questions 'who?', 'what?', 'when?', 'where?' and 'why?'
- Main body of text then retells the events in chronological order
- Ends with a conclusion that briefly summarises the text or comments on the event

Linguistic features

- Past tense
- First person (personal recounts) or third person (impersonal)
- Focuses on named individuals or participants
- Use of time connectives to aid chronological order (firstly, afterwards, meanwhile, subsequently, finally)
- Often contains interesting details to bring incidents alive to the reader

Examples of recount texts

- newspaper reports
- diary entries
- letters
- write-up of trips or activities
- autobiographies/biographies

Teaching recount writing

At first glance, recounts seem to be relatively straightforward; after all, children seem to get plenty of practice doing their 'news' writing at school! However, as with any retelling, it is easy for children to neglect to include vital pieces of information. The knowledge of the event is in the children's heads and it is our job, as teachers, to make sure that that knowledge is shared with the reader in order to make the event purposeful for them. Children tend to list events, as if on a timeline, but they need to include specific information and use relevant connectives so that the reader is able to have all the information needed to imagine themselves there.

Many children need a lot of support in organising the information chronologically. A flow chart is a useful tool to enable children to sequence events in the correct order. It also enables them to see where there are natural divisions for paragraphs. A word bank of time connectives could also prove useful.

Encourage the children to organise the planning of their recount by listing information under the headings: who, what, when, where and why. This will ensure they include all the vital information.

Recount writing – progression

Simple recounts are introduced in Key Stage 1 (Reception: T15; Year 1, Term 3: T20).

In Year 3 children experiment with recounting the same event in a variety of ways, such as a story, a letter or a newspaper report (Term 3: T22).

In Year 4 children examine opening sentences that set scenes and capture interest and identify the key features of newspapers (Term 1: T18, T20). They write newspaper style reports (Term 1: T24). They learn to make short notes (Term 2: T21).

In Year 5 (Term 1: T21, T23, T24, T26) children learn to identify the features of recounted texts such as sports reports and diaries and to write recounts based on subject, topic or personal experiences for different audiences. They discuss the purpose of note taking and how this influences the nature of the notes made.

In **Year 6** (Term 1: T11, T14, T15, T16; Term 3: T19, T22) children are reading to distinguish between biography and autobiography and are developing the skills of biographical and autobiographical writing in role. They review a range of text features and select the appropriate style and form to suit a specific purpose and audience.

Unit 1

Lesson focus

Religious Education Unit 6A – Worship and community

Overall aim

To analyse the main features of a recount and to write a personal recount of a visit to a Christian church.

Religious Education emphasis

In this unit the children are encouraged to perceive themselves as members of their communities. This entails learning about different communities and how those communities' beliefs shape their behaviour. By studying beliefs and behaviour, the children can begin to understand the link between them. This can lead to them realising how their own behaviour can be an expression of their own beliefs, whether these are religious or not.

Literacy links

Revision of Year 5, Term 1: T21, T24

About this unit

In this unit the children will learn about the daily activities of a vicar of a Christian church. They will find out how a vicar is a part of different communities and relate this to their own lives. They will learn about the features of recounts in order to write their own recount about a visit to a Christian church.

Switching on

Learning objectives

- To make notes.
- To find out about the activities and roles undertaken by a vicar of a Christian church.

Resources

- Sheets B, C and D (pages 12–15)

What to do

Tell the children that they are going to explore how a vicar's faith directs his life and the role he plays in the community. Tell them that they are also going to explore how the church, for which he is a minister, reflects the needs of the community he serves.

Share an enlarged version of Sheet B. Explain that the text is part of an autobiography written by the Reverend Carr. Discuss the meaning of the word 'autobiography' and compare it with a biography. Ask them if they have read an autobiography before. Read through the text, asking some of the children to read out different paragraphs. Ask them which communities they think the

vicar belongs to (his family, the church, the school, the village, the chapter group, the prayer group and so on). Write these on the board.

Then ask the children to work in pairs and read through the recount again in order to find examples of the things the vicar does because it is his job as a vicar (such as, editing the parish magazine, daily prayers for peace, looking at headstones). Explain to them that these will be his official duties linked to his religious (Christian) community.

Then ask them to list the things he does that are not part of his official duties. Ask them to list them under the headings 'Family', 'School', 'Village' and 'Other'.

When they have finished, discuss with them if they think his religious beliefs direct his actions in each category. (The children may have different opinions about this. For example, some may feel that his actions for his family are not specifically directed by his religious beliefs. If this is the case, you could suggest to them that a main Christian belief is that Jesus said that people should love and serve one another and that Christians take this as a code of conduct for themselves. Explain that people do not have to be Christian to also believe in behaving this way, but the vicar may be using this Christian belief in his everyday conduct towards those around him.)

Discuss also the concept that the vicar belongs to a small community – his family – but that he also belongs to communities that become wider and wider. For example, he belongs to the school community and the village community. He also belongs to a group of clergymen from other communities. He also has links with religious communities in Sussex and London. Explain to the children that belonging to communities is a bit like a throwing a pebble into a pond, the circles it makes become wider and wider. Discuss with them how the vicar's membership of smaller and larger communities could be illustrated (for example, by widening circles, by a web and so on). Ask them to produce a diagrammatic representation of the communities the vicar belongs to.

Plenary

Share what they found out and how they represented it. Explain that diagrams are a very useful way of making notes. Ask them if they are in the same position as the vicar (having different circles of communities) and discuss how far their membership of communities reaches.

Then hand out copies of Sheets C and D. Ask one child to call out an item from Sheet C (such as 'lectern') and ask another child to read the description/explanation from Sheet D.

Ask them to list the times and events when the vicar's village community may use the church. Ask them how they think the building reflects the religious needs and beliefs of the community (for example, the spire as a focal point in the locality, the layout reflecting the shape of the cross and so on).

Revving up

Learning objectives

■ To investigate the key features of a personal recount text.

Resources

■ Sheet B (pages 12 and 13)

What to do

Remind the children about the text they shared in the previous lesson. Tell them that the text is an autobiographical recount. Ask them to tell you what a recount is. Write their ideas on the board. Explain that they are going to explore the features of a recount in detail by looking at Sheet B again. If appropriate explain that 'structural' features are how the text is organised and put together and 'linguistic' features refers to the type of words and phrases that are used.

Provide the children with their own copy of Sheet B. They could work in pairs. Explain that the purpose of a recount text is to inform and entertain the reader. Ask them to find five examples of places where information is given (for example, a vicar's day begins with prayer, a vicar attends services outside his own parish and a vicar often has links with the local school) and underline them in red. Share what they found out. Then ask them to underline in blue examples where the author has tried to entertain his readers (such as descriptions of his everyday life or his responses to his walk with the dogs). Share what they found out.

Write on the board the following structural features: 'introduction', 'chronologically organised paragraphs' and 'conclusion'. Explain to the children what the terms mean. (The introduction explains to the reader what the recount is going to be about, chronologically organised paragraphs retell the events in the order in which they happened at the time and a conclusion sums up what has been said and redirects the reader to the theme of the recount.)

Reread the introduction and the conclusion together. Do the children think the text matches the description of an introduction and a conclusion? Next, ask them to label the introductory and concluding paragraphs and then number the other paragraphs as 'Event no 1', 'Event no 2' and so on.

When they have finished, discuss what the effect would be if the recount text was not organised chronologically.

Now tell them that they are going to investigate the linguistic features of a recount text. Explain that, as a recount is a retelling of something that has already happened, it is written in the past tense. Ask them to give you some examples of verbs written in the past tense and then to find some in the text. Write 'verbs – past tense' on the board.

Tell the children that a personal recount text is a retelling by the person who experienced the events and so uses personalised or first person sentence structures. Explain that this means that 'I', 'my', 'we' and 'our' will often be used. On the board, write 'first person'.

Explain that a recount will use time connectives. Remind them that a connective is a word or phrase that links either different parts of a sentence together or links ideas between sentences together. Remind them that a time connective will be a word or phrase that suggests time is passing. Provide examples from the text (for example, 'after', 'on my return', 'when' and 'while'). On the board, write 'time connectives'.

Tell the children that you now want them to work in pairs to find examples of the three linguistic features listed. They need to use different colours for each feature and underline or circle the feature when they find it.

While the majority of children are doing this, sit with a group and do guided reading for time connectives. Reiterate to them what a time connective is and remind them that it can be a word or a phrase. If they are less able, provide them with the following list to find and underline: after, on my return, when, at about, while, next, later and finally.

Tell them that other examples of time connectives would be: subsequently, before, soon, in a second, now.

Plenary

Ask the group you have been working with to give examples of time connectives they have found in Sheet B to the rest of the class. Ask these children to give the rest of the class the other examples you provided. Write up all the examples of time connectives on the board and ask the children to copy any down that they do not already know.

Before the next lesson arrange for the children to visit a Christian church. Ask them to make notes about the special features of the church (as listed on Sheet C) and find out about how it is used by the community.

Taking off

Learning objectives

■ To plan a personal recount.

Resources

■ Sheets A, C, D and E (pages 10 and 11 and 14–16)
■ The children's notes from the visit to the church

What to do

Note: before this lesson, the children should have visited a Christian church.

Tell the children that today they are going to plan their recount of their visit to the Christian church. Remind them that a recount is a retelling of an experience and its purpose is to inform and entertain the reader. Refer back to the 'Revving up' lesson and ask them if they can remember any of the structural and linguistic features of a recount text. Write their ideas on the board and add any that have been forgotten. Use an enlarged version of Sheet A to do this.

Tell the children that you are going to help them write their own recount by writing an example for them. What follows is for your eyes only, for you to use or adapt as you wish. What you say, as if to yourself, is written in italics; what you write is written in bold.

The first thing I need to do is make an opening statement or introduction that will tell the reader what the recount text is about. Well, it is about a visit to a Christian church. If I just wrote that, it wouldn't be very interesting, so I should add a bit of detail to entertain the reader.

On a bright sunny morning, our class met at school to get ready for our visit to (name of church) **Church in** (name village or town). **We were going to the church to explore the building and grounds. We wanted to find out how the church helped Christian people worship and how it had a place in their lives.**

Let me look at that. I have made it clear what the recount is going to be about and I have given the reader a bit of description of what the weather was like, which adds a bit of interest. I have also told the reader the purpose of our visit. I have used the past tense; for example, I have written 'met' the past tense of 'meet'. I have used the first person; for example, I have written 'we' and 'our'. I don't seem to have used a time connective. Let me try now.

After we had collected all we needed, we began to walk to the church. I felt happy as we walked along because it was nice to get out of the classroom and I was looking forward to the work we would do in the church and the churchyard.

Good, I have kept all the features there, I have used a time connective by writing 'after' and I have given an idea of my responses to the trip, which is always entertaining for the reader. It wouldn't do to give descriptions and my responses every time, though, and I haven't yet used any vocabulary that will inform the reader. Let me try a different sort of paragraph. I shall keep the events in chronological order, but this time I shall give information and not give a description or my responses. I can add more of those in later paragraphs.

I could see the spire of the church ahead of us. The spire of a church is high so that people in the local community can easily see where the church is when they wish to go to church. Sometimes, the spire will hold bells that will ring out to call people to services or to celebrate an event, like a wedding. We turned the corner and saw the church ahead of us. The vicar was waiting for us at the door.

I am happy with this now. I have kept the recount moving forwards as the events took place. I have given some information and used the correct vocabulary by writing 'spire'. If I carried on writing, I would try to inform my reader by using the correct words for parts of the church and I would explain what they mean. I would try to entertain my reader by giving some descriptions and some of my responses. I would keep all the other features going too, like using the past tense, putting the events in chronological order, using some temporal connectives, making it personal and finishing with a closing statement.

Ask the children to go through the structural and linguistic features you have incorporated. Then ask them if they could improve your writing in any way. Discuss their responses and change any part you agree on as an improvement.

Provide the children with a copy of Sheet E. Explain that they can use this to make notes in order to plan their recount. Tell them that you want them to write ideas for their opening statement (introduction) and closing statement (conclusion) and that they should choose several events/topics from their visit that they wish to recount. Remind them about how the events in a recount are organised chronologically. Tell them that each event will become a paragraph in the recount.

Next, explain to the children how to complete the event boxes on Sheet E in order to help them plan each paragraph:

1. Event – write the event/topic you want to write about;
2. Vocabulary – write some words that relate to this. Use Sheets C and D to help here as well as the notes from the visit;
3. Explanation – write the function of the part of the Church;
4. Description – describe anything that caught your attention;
5. Response – write how you felt, what your opinion was;
6. Time connective – write a time connective to link the paragraph. (Explain that they don't have to give a connective for every event.)

Explain that Sheet E is for making notes and planning their recount texts. They do not need to recount every event but choose what they consider the most important events of the visit. Tell them that at this stage they simply need to record what they plan to write their responses to, rather than give their responses. For example: response – headstones.

Move around the classroom while the children are completing Sheet E, ensuring that they have understood the need for notes and that no children are attempting to write things out in full.

Plenary

Ask the children for examples of their planning. Discuss the events they have chosen to recount. Choose one of the events mentioned and share ideas about how this event could be written in full so that the reader is informed and entertained.

Flying solo

Learning objectives

■ To write a personal recount.

Resources

■ Sheet E (page 16) already completed by the children

What to do

Tell the children that today they are going to write their recount using their planning sheet (Sheet E). Ask them to work in pairs to read through their plans. Tell them to help each other by discussing the events chosen to remind themselves of what happened and to check their plans to ensure that they have planned sufficient information to write their recounts. (For example, has their partner written down a few time connectives to use? Has their partner jotted down the events in the order in which they happened? Has their partner used the correct vocabulary that describes what is inside the church?)

Explain that they are to going to use their notes on the sheet to write complete sentences. Use one child's sheet to model how to do this.

Tell the children that they can draw diagrams and pictures to illustrate their recount, but that these will have to be done after they have finished writing.

Allow plenty of time for this activity. Ensure that the environment is quiet so that the children are not disturbed and have time to think and write. While the children are doing this, help any children who need support.

If possible, take some time to write a recount of the visit yourself. It is very beneficial for the children to see you writing as they write.

Plenary

If you had time to begin your own recount, read this out to the children, discussing any difficulties or successes you had. Ask them if they had any similar experiences while they were writing. (The children will learn the thinking and writing process from sharing with you the writing experience.)

Ask a child to read out their recount. Comment on the positive features they have incorporated.

title
to say what
the recount is
about

A day in my life
by the Reverend Alan Carr

Having Christian beliefs and being a vicar in a small village in Sussex affects my life and actions. I will tell you about an ordinary day in my life so that you can see what I do when it is not Sunday.

introduction
to orientate
the reader

past
tense

On Thursday, 27th March, 2003, I woke up at 6.30am, had a wash and got dressed so that I would be ready for my morning prayer time, which I do every day. Sometimes I do a prayer time in the choir stalls in the church, but this morning I decided to go to my study. I sat cross legged on the carpet and opened my prayer book. My prayer book is a mixture of scripture, psalms and prayers and there is a prayer for every day.

time
connective

After I had said my prayers, I had breakfast and walked the 400 metres to the church to open it so that others could come in and pray if they wished to. There are five of us in my family and my wife goes out to work, so on my return I helped get the children ready for school and college. When everyone had gone, I took our dogs for a walk across the fields. The sun was shining and there was still dew on the grass which made the morning feel fresh and sparkling. There were signs of spring to look at everywhere, but there was work to be done back at the vicarage.

At about 9.30am I started work in my study. Today I was editing a special article for the parish magazine about the anniversary of the death of St Richard of Chichester, the patron saint of Sussex.

first
person

I am going to a memorial service at Westminster Abbey in London soon. This is for a person who lived in the village, so I wrote letters and rang people about this service. While I was in the middle of writing a letter, the doorbell rang. It was someone who wanted to talk about a funeral service happening tomorrow. The lady who died had lived in the village all her life. We discussed who would do the readings and what would happen during the service. When my visitor had left, I just had time for a quick cup of coffee as I was due to go down to the village school and take an assembly there.

information
organised in
paragraphs in
chronological
order

Sipping my coffee, I thought about what I would say in assembly. It is Mothering Sunday in a few days time, so I decided to talk about this. The children were sitting quietly when I arrived in the school hall. I told them the story 'I Want My Mummy' by Alan and Janet Ahlberg. They thought it was very funny. I want the children to enjoy my assemblies, but I also want to give them a Christian message at the same time.

Leaving the school, I went to the village post office and bought a card for Mothering Sunday and some Euros for my son who is going to France soon. I chatted to some villagers about the lovely weather and asked about the health of someone who had been sick. I returned home. A man showed up to fix my printing machine and the postman arrived. I began to sort through my letters.

At about 12 o'clock, I walked back down to the church because we are having daily prayers for peace in the church because of the war in Iraq. It was then time

for me to walk round the churchyard with the church warden to look at the headstones of the people buried there. The headstones date from 1662 to 2003. Many of the family names have relatives still living in the village. Someone in the local council wants us to straighten the headstones, but we checked and they are quite safe.

After lunch my son came home from college so I gave him a driving lesson. Then I sat in the garden for a while, fed the dogs and put the washing on the line. I had half an hour, so I popped down to say goodbye to an old lady who has always lived in the village and who is moving to a nursing home in London next week.

My next port of call was a nearby village. I drove over there for our weekly 'Chapter meeting'. This is a gathering of local clergymen. We share news, pray together and have tea and coffee. It was four o'clock by the time the meeting was over, so I went home and prepared dinner. The children returned home from school and at 5.30pm we had our family meal.

A couple who are planning to get married arrived at 7pm to talk to me about preparing for marriage. We talked about the spiritual meaning of marriage and discussed the hymns and music for their wedding and if they wanted the bells rung.

Later, at eight o'clock, there was a prayer study meeting. At these, a group of Christians gather together to read, study and think about the Bible.

Finally, at 10pm, I sat down and watched the news about the war. I said my final prayers of the day and went to bed.

My beliefs and my life as a vicar in a small community affect most of what I do. I meet many people belonging to different communities in my daily life, but not all of them are related to the Church. However, through prayer and my actions I try to look after the spiritual welfare of myself and my parishioners. The Church is central to my life.

A day in my life
by the Reverend Alan Carr

Having Christian beliefs and being a vicar in a small village in Sussex affects my life and actions. I will tell you about an ordinary day in my life so that you can see what I do when it is not Sunday.

On Thursday, 27th March, 2003, I woke up at 6.30am, had a wash and got dressed so that I would be ready for my morning prayer time, which I do every day. Sometimes I do a prayer time in the choir stalls in the church, but this morning I decided to go to my study. I sat cross legged on the carpet and opened my prayer book. My prayer book is a mixture of scripture, psalms and prayers and there is a prayer for every day.

After I had said my prayers, I had breakfast and walked the 400 metres to the church to open it so that others could come in and pray if they wished to. There are five of us in my family and my wife goes out to work, so on my return I helped get the children ready for school and college. When everyone had gone, I took our dogs for a walk across the fields. The sun was shining and there was still dew on the grass which made the morning feel fresh and sparkling. There were signs of spring to look at everywhere, but there was work to be done back at the vicarage.

At about 9.30am I started work in my study. Today I was editing a special article for the parish magazine about the anniversary of the death of St Richard of Chichester, the patron saint of Sussex.

I am going to a memorial service at Westminster Abbey in London soon. This is for a person who lived in the village, so I wrote letters and rang people about this service. While I was in the middle of writing a letter, the doorbell rang. It was someone who wanted to talk about a funeral service happening tomorrow. The lady who died had lived in the village all her life. We discussed who would do the readings and what would happen during the service. When my visitor had left, I just had time for a quick cup of coffee as I was due to go down to the village school and take an assembly there.

Sipping my coffee, I thought about what I would say in assembly. It is Mothering Sunday in a few days time, so I decided to talk about this. The children were sitting quietly when I arrived in the school hall. I told them the story 'I Want My Mummy' by Alan and Janet Ahlberg. They thought it was very funny. I want the children to enjoy my assemblies, but I also want to give them a Christian message at the same time.

Leaving the school, I went to the village post office and bought a card for Mothering Sunday and some Euros for my son who is going to France soon. I chatted to some villagers about the lovely weather and asked about the health of someone who had been sick. I returned home. A man showed up to fix my printing machine and the postman arrived. I began to sort through my letters.

At about 12 o'clock, I walked back down to the church because we are having daily prayers for peace in the church because of the war in Iraq. It was then time for me to walk round the churchyard with the church warden to look at the headstones of the people buried there. The headstones date from 1662 to 2003. Many of the family names have relatives still living in the village. Someone in the local council wants us to straighten the headstones, but we checked and they are quite safe.

After lunch my son came home from college so I gave him a driving lesson. Then I sat in the garden for a while, fed the dogs and put the washing on the line. I had half an hour, so I popped down to say goodbye to an old lady who has always lived in the village and who is moving to a nursing home in London next week.

My next port of call was a nearby village. I drove over there for our weekly 'Chapter meeting'. This is a gathering of local clergymen. We share news, pray together and have tea and coffee. It was four o'clock by the time the meeting was over, so I went home and prepared dinner. The children returned home from school and at 5.30pm we had our family meal.

A couple who are planning to get married arrived at 7pm to talk to me about preparing for marriage. We talked about the spiritual meaning of marriage and discussed the hymns and music for their wedding and if they wanted the bells rung.

Later, at eight o'clock, there was a prayer study meeting. At these, a group of Christians gather together to read, study and think about the Bible.

Finally, at 10pm, I sat down and watched the news about the war. I said my final prayers of the day and went to bed.

My beliefs and my life as a vicar in a small community affect most of what I do. I meet many people belonging to different communities in my daily life, but not all of them are related to the Church. However, through prayer and my actions I try to look after the spiritual welfare of myself and my parishioners. The Church is central to my life.

Sheet C

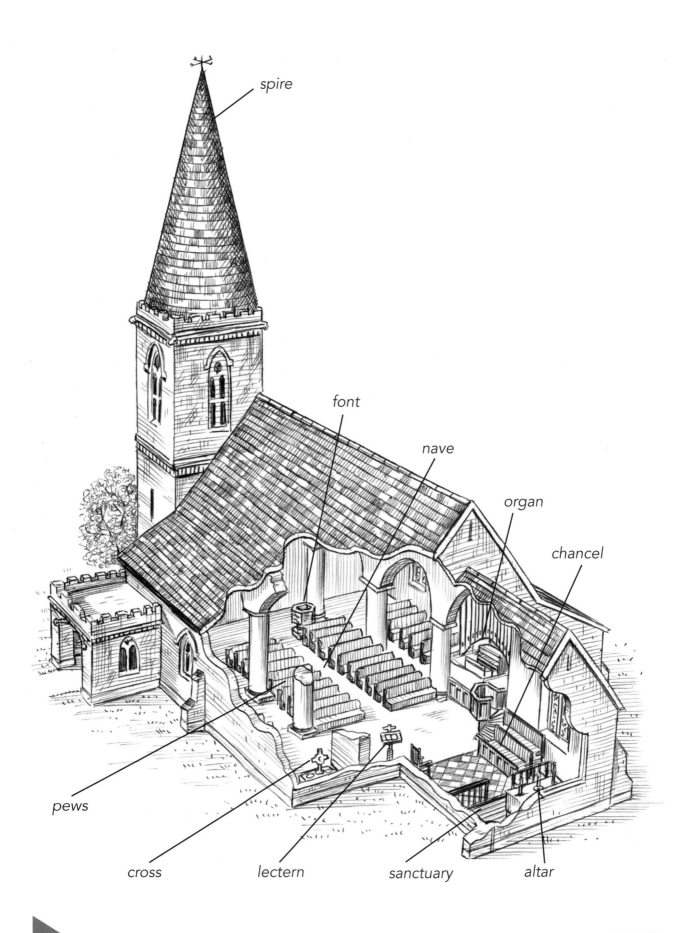

spire

font

nave

organ

chancel

pews

cross

lectern

sanctuary

altar

Altar – a table that reminds the Christian community of the table that Jesus used at the last supper.

Chancel – part of the church where the altar stands. It is used by anyone who has an official part to play in the services, such as the priest or vicar or the choir.

Cross – the symbol of the Christian religion. A Christian church is laid out in a cross, to remind us of the cross of Jesus.

Font – a container for water where babies are christened. Christenings are a child's entry into the Christian community of the church and the fonts are often placed near the entrance to a church to show this.

Lectern – a reading desk where the Bible is held. The vicar or priest will read parts of the Bible to the congregation from here.

Nave – the walkway through the middle of the church. It is part of the cross shape of the church.

Pews – wooden benches where the Christian community or congregation sit during services.

Pulpit – a raised platform where the vicar or priest will deliver the sermon to the congregation. It is high so that the vicar or priest can be seen by the congregation. The sermon will be a talk about what has been read from the Bible, explaining the message and encouraging the congregation to behave in a Christian way in their everyday lives.

Sanctuary – place that is recognised as holy and is often in the innermost part of the church, within the altar rails. In olden days, people who were in trouble with the law or others could go here and be safe.

Spire – a tall, slender part of the church that tapers to a point. It is tall so that everyone in the community can see where the church is. It often contains a bell tower that will ring to call people to a service or to celebrate an event, such as a wedding.

Sheet E

Title

Introduction or opening statement	Event 1: Vocabulary: Explanation? Description? Response? Time connective:
Event 2: Vocabulary: Explanation? Description? Response? Time connective:	Event 3: Vocabulary: Explanation? Description? Response? Time connective:
Event 4: Vocabulary: Explanation? Description? Response? Time connective:	Event 5: Vocabulary: Explanation? Description? Response? Time connective:
Event 6: Vocabulary: Explanation? Description? Response? Time connective:	Conclusion or closing statement

Unit 2

Lesson focus

History Unit 20 – What can we learn about recent history from studying the life of a famous person?

Overall aim

To analyse the main features of a newspaper recount and to write a newspaper recount about the death of John Lennon.

History emphasis

In this unit the children learn the key skills of finding information from a variety of sources. As the unit is concerned with recent history, they may have the unusual opportunity of using primary sources by interviewing and talking to people who have lived through these times. The children are given the opportunity to evaluate the sources of information.

Literacy links

Year 6, Term 1: T11, T12, T15, T16

About this unit

In this unit the children examine a key event in recent history, identify and describe the event and then select and organise information to create their newspaper recount. The children will also be asked to differentiate between fact and opinion. Learning about the opinions of people who lived at a certain time allows them insight into their ideas, beliefs and attitudes.

Switching on

Learning objectives

■ To understand the differences between 'fact' and 'opinion'.
■ To gather information about the death of John Lennon.

Resources

■ Sheets A, B, C and D (pages 23–26)

What to do

Note: before this lesson, the children should have already learned about the life of John Lennon.

Tell the children that today they are going to find out about the death of John Lennon. Divide them into groups and share out copies of Sheets A, B, C and D between them. (For example, one group may have Sheet A, another group Sheet B and so on. It may be useful to give Sheets A and B to less able groups.) Explain that you want each group to read through their sheet and then spend time preparing to read it out to the rest of the class. The groups can decide how to do this; for example, each person could read one part each.

After about ten minutes, ask each group to read their sheet to the class. When all the items have been read out, have a general discussion about what they have found out about the death of John Lennon. (You do not need to go into too much detail yet because the texts will be explored in more detail.) Tell them that Sheet C is from a local newspaper and Sheet D a national one. Do they notice any differences between them?

Tell the children that they are now going to investigate the differences between fact and opinion in the pieces of text they have just read. Explain that a fact is something that cannot be disproved. Provide examples by pointing out facts within the classroom (for example, the time, the number of children present, the colour of their jumpers). Explain that an opinion is what people think about things and, as such, there may be as many different opinions as there are people. Provide examples (such as 'there are too many children in the class, this class could have more children in it' and 'I like the colours of your jumper, I don't like the colour of your jumper'). Ask the children to give you examples of facts and opinions themselves.

Hand out a copy of Sheet A to all the children in the class. Ask them to give you a fact (for example, 'In 1970 the Beatles broke up.') and an opinion (for example, 'They said that John Lennon created the mood of the time.').

Hand out a copy of Sheet C to all the children. Read out the first three paragraphs. Point out that the first paragraph contains facts and the second paragraph contains a mixture of facts and opinion (opinion: 'the founder and driving force behind the legendary Beatles'). Ask them to look at the third paragraph to identify the opinion ('a local screwball with no apparent motive for shooting Lennon'). Ask them if they can rephrase this paragraph leaving out the opinion (for example, 'the Police said someone had been charged with the murder of John Lennon').

Explain that reports in the media should be honest and fair. Ask them if they think this is always the case. Return to the third paragraph in Sheet C. Tell them that when this report was written, the man who killed John Lennon had not yet been tried for his murder and no one knew much about him. Ask them if they think describing him as 'a local screwball' would affect public opinion and if it could affect the fairness of his trial.

Return to the second paragraph of Sheet C. Ask the children what the other Beatles might have to say about the opinion that John Lennon was the 'driving force' behind the Beatles. Explain that for a report to be honest and fair, the facts should be stated clearly and the opinions given should reflect more than one point of view, preferably giving opposing points of view. Refer to paragraphs 24 (A spokesperson for Wessex…) and 25 (But Mr Pete Dolan…) to illustrate this point.

Tell the children that they are now going to go through the Sheets A, C and D to divide the facts from the opinions (hand out a copy of Sheet D to all the class). Tell them that they are going to divide the facts and opinions in the following way:

1. Sheet A can be cut up and divided into two piles, 'fact' and 'opinion';

2. Examples of opinions from Sheets C and D can be copied out or highlighted, the rest can be assumed to be factual.

(Each child should be offered some way of keeping these items together at the end of the lesson in order to be retrieved at a later lesson. This could be a plastic wallet or a piece of sugar paper folded over with the child's name on the front.)

As the children are doing this, sit with a group of children for a guided reading session. Begin with Sheet A and discuss each part, asking them if it is a fact or opinion. If the group is less able, move on to use Sheet C and help them find the opinions in the report. If the children are more able, use Sheet D for this activity.

Plenary

Share what the children have found out. Do they agree on what is fact and what is opinion? Were they aware that newspaper reports contained both facts and opinions? How might this affect the way they read the stories in newspapers?

As a homework task, ask the children to find out if any of their family or friends remember the event of the death of John Lennon. Ask them to find out what they thought about the event and how it affected people at that time.

Revving up

Learning objective

■ To explore the key features of a newspaper recount.

Resources

■ Sheets C and D (pages 25 and 26)

What to do

Tell the children that today they are going to investigate the key features of a journalistic report so that they can plan and write a similar report in future lessons. Explain that a newspaper report is actually a recount because it is a retelling of events that have happened.

Ask them to refer to their copies of Sheet C from the previous lesson. Look at the heading. Explain that a heading in a newspaper report is called 'the headline'. Ask them to tell you how this particular headline might grab the attention of the reader. Point out the size and type of the font (large and bold).

Write this sentence on the board: 'A madman gunned down John Lennon, a former member of the Beatles'.

Ask the children what words are missing from the headline. Which version is more likely to catch the attention of the reader – the headline in the newspaper or the sentence on the board? Ask them why they think the newspaper headline is more 'catchy' (it is much briefer, it is more like a verbal 'shout'). Ask the children to point out the different tenses used ('guns down' and 'gunned down'). Explain that using the present tense makes the headline sound more immediate – as if it is happening now, which creates for the reader a dramatic feeling of urgency.

Turn to the headline on Sheet D. Ask the children to provide you with suggestions for a full sentence for this headline.

Explain that a journalistic report will begin with an opening that tells the reader what it is going to be about. It explains who, what, when, where and why. Ask a child to read the first paragraph from both reports. Ask if they tell the reader what the report is going to be about.

Explain that a journalistic report will then provide paragraphs that are linked together to inform the reader of different aspects of the subject. Refer to Sheet C and help the children decide on the different aspects; that is:

Paragraphs 3–5: Mark Chapman.

Paragraphs 6–9: Chronological reporting of events.

Paragraphs 10–14: Yoko Ono's responses and John's medical treatment.

Paragraphs 15–20: Review of John's life and opinions.

Paragraphs 21–28: Cashing in on John's death.

Point out that although this report is about the death of John Lennon, it also provides the reader with extra, interesting information that incorporates the life of John Lennon and the effect his death has had on some people. Explain that the reporters select information that they feel will be interesting to the reader.

Ask the children to work in small groups and read the report on Sheet D. Ask them to identify the following different aspects of this report: the mourners, Lennon's life, the events, Mark Chapman, grief, America as a violent place, links with the assassination of President Kennedy. When they have finished this, point out that the paragraphs are organised in such a way that one aspect is covered before the reporter moves on to another.

Tell the children that another key feature of a journalistic report is the use of emotive, entertaining language. Return their attention to the headlines. Ask them which words or phrases stand out as different to everyday language (for example, 'madman', 'guns', 'wave of grief').

Write this sentence on the board: 'People were very upset over John Lennon's murder'. Explain that 'wave of grief' conveys a more dramatic feeling to the reader than the sentence on the board. Explain that this headline is more exciting and will therefore grab the readers' attention and encourage them to buy the newspaper.

Ask them to work in pairs to highlight any language they find in the reports that they think is dramatic, over emotional or exciting. It may be useful to give lower ability children Sheet C and higher ability children Sheet D.

Sit with a group of children and help them to find some emotive language. Discuss the findings, asking them why they think the words and phrases used will be more interesting to the reader than more everyday language would be.

Plenary

Ask the children to tell you what they have learned about the special features of a journalistic report. Share their ideas.

Write the following on the board:

Today the children in Class 6 were visited by an alien. The alien had green hair, three heads and was approximately two feet high. The children asked the alien many questions before the alien became tired and made a few of them disappear.

Ask the children to add words or phrases that would make this passage more exciting as a newspaper report and then write a catchy headline.

Taking off

Learning objective

■ To plan a newspaper recount.

Resources

■ Sheets A, B, C and D (pages 23–26)

What to do

Tell the children that today they are going to plan their own newspaper recount about the death of John Lennon. Tell them that you are going to model writing the beginning of the report. The following is for your eyes only to use or adapt as you wish. What you say is written in italics, what you write is written in bold.

What do I need to write a journalistic report? I need a catchy headline. (Write 'catchy headline' on the board.) I need facts. (Write 'facts' on the board.) I need opinions. (Write 'opinions'.) I need exciting language. (Write 'exciting language'.) I need to select the information I think will interest the reader. (Write 'select for interest'.) I need to organise my facts and opinions so that an aspect of the subject is put together. (Write 'organise aspects'.)

Fine, now I have a list I can check as I go along. What's the first thing? Oh yes, a catchy headline. What is my report going to be about? The murder of John Lennon. Let me think… I'll try this:

MURDER, MADNESS – LENNON DIES!

I've got a nice bit of alliteration there – murder and madness both beginning with 'm'. I've put the headline in capitals, I've made it short and it sounds dramatic. What's next? An opening to tell the reader what the report is about. I need some facts here. Who, what, where, when, how? Right.

John Lennon was killed outside his apartment block in New York last night. Mark Chapman, reported to be a fan of John Lennon, shot the ex-Beatle a few hours after asking for his autograph.

Now what? I could pop in an opinion here. Let me look through my pile of opinions. Ah yes, in the 'Bath Chronicle' report there is the opinion of the police that Chapman is a screwball. Well, I can't copy that, but I can put it in my own words.

Chapman is said by police to be someone who is crazy and there does not appear to be any real motive for the shooting.

What now? Exciting language – well, let me add some more information and include some really dramatic language. Looking at my list on the board, I have to select information I think is going to interest the reader and organise it so that an aspect of the subject is put together. I think at this point, the reader will want to know how the events happened. I'll start with Chapman asking John Lennon for his autograph earlier in the day. That's really spooky.

Earlier in the day, John and Yoko had left their luxurious apartment to go to a recording studio. Among the fans waiting peacefully outside was John's insane killer. Little did Lennon know, as he smiled kindly at Chapman and gave him his autograph, that a few hours later this ordinary looking man would pull out a gun and blast away John's life.

Now, looking at that last paragraph I have given facts, provided opinion such as 'insane killer' and 'ordinary looking man'. I have selected the aspect I want to write about that will interest the reader. I have also used very dramatic language, such as 'blast away John's life'.

Now turn to the children and ask them for their opinions. Go through the checklist on the board and ask them to provide you with evidence in your writing that you have covered these features.

Tell them that they are now going to plan their reports. Tell them that you will help them by putting on the board the order their reports will be in. Write on the board:

Heading

Opening

Events of the killing

Mark Chapman

John Lennon's life

People's response to the killing.

Tell the children that you will give them five minutes to work in pairs to come up with a good headline. When they have finished, ask for some examples.

Then give them five minutes to work in pairs to come up with a short paragraph that tells the reader what the report is going to be about. When they have finished, ask for some examples from around the class.

Now tell them that they are to go through all the resources and select the information and opinions they want to use for the rest of the list on the board. Tell them to head a piece of paper for each part of the list (for example, 'events of the killing') and write the information and opinions they have selected in note form that go with the headings they have written. Remind them that they are not to copy out whole sections of text, as their final reports must be their own work. They are to just jot down a few words as if they were reporters, to help them to write their reports at the next lesson. Encourage them to use more than one source.

Sit with a group of less able children during this part of the lesson. Encourage them to do each part of the list in sequence. Assist them in finding information and opinions at each stage. Ensure they are using notes, rather than copying out whole sections of text.

Plenary

Ask a child to read out their notes for the events of the killing. Ask the class for suggestions on how part of this could be rewritten in full using their own words. Write their suggestions on the board. Remind the children of the use of language to excite and interest the reader.

Flying solo

Learning objective

■ To write a newspaper recount.

Resources

■ Planning from previous lesson
■ Thesauruses

What to do

Tell the children that they are now going to use their plans to write their newspaper report on the death of John Lennon.

Ask them to work in pairs and go through their headings, opening paragraphs and planning. They should help each other by asking the following questions, which can be written on the board:

■ Is the headline short and catchy?
■ Does the opening paragraph inform the reader what the report is about?
■ Have they got their planning sheets in order (events, Mark Chapman, John Lennon's life, people's responses)?
■ Have they got a selection of facts and opinions?

After they have done this, refer back to the 'Revving up' lesson and remind them of the need to use exciting and dramatic language. Tell them that while they are writing they can use a thesaurus to help them choose words that are not 'everyday' words.

Remind them that the purpose of writing a journalistic report is to ensure that people buy the newspaper, so their reports should be factual and contain opinions, but must be designed to interest the reader.

Remind them that they are working from notes and that their writing should be an expansion of these notes, written in their own words, in full sentences.

Allow the children plenty of time for writing their reports. If it is possible, a suitable ICT program could be used to present their work like a newspaper report. The environment should be quiet so that they are able to think, organise and write.

If some children need to be supported throughout the writing process, this can be done in a variety of ways:

1. You could act as a scribe for the children;
2. The children could first verbalise their ideas to you, then reshape them for writing;
3. The children could work in pairs, assisting each other;
4. A group of children could work together to each produce a section or aspect of the report, putting them together when they have finished.

Plenary

Ask the children if they have gathered any ideas about the significance of John Lennon in society from the reporting and language used in the report of his death and the responses of people after his death.

In 1970 the Beatles broke up. John went to live in New York with Yoko Ono. They lived in the Dakota building. During the 70s John and Yoko made many films and songs protesting against war and violence. In 1975 their son, Sean, was born.

John stayed at home and looked after Sean. Yoko Ono took over managing their business affairs. In 1980, John came out of retirement to make an album.

John Lennon is reported to have said 'Don't expect John Lennon or Yoko Ono or Bob Dylan or Jesus to come down and help you live. You have to do it for yourself'.

John Lennon said that he wanted to die before Yoko Ono as he didn't think he could cope without her.

Mark Chapman, the man who killed John Lennon in 1980, travelled from his home in Hawaii two weeks before he shot John Lennon. He was already planning to kill him.

John Lennon was stalked for three days by his killer.

Mark Chapman claims to have no recollection of killing John Lennon.

Within a couple of hours after the shooting, there was bedlam outside the Dakota building. Fans carried candles and sang John's song 'Give Peace a Chance'.

The next day, the Dakota building had become a shrine. Hundreds of mourners chanted John's other song 'All you need is love.' Radios played non-stop Beatles music.

The news was broadcast all over the world.

Everyone paid tributes to John Lennon. Even presidents of America. They said that John Lennon created the mood of the time. Other people praised his brilliant poetry, his humour, his ability to convey his great rage against injustice, his rock and roll and surreal songs.

Some people pointed out that John Lennon had died violently, like many other people of peace.

His son, Sean, was supposed to have asked his mother why Mark Chapman killed his daddy if he was a fan. Yoko Ono is said to have replied that Mark Chapman was a confused man.

Yoko Ono decided against having a funeral for John Lennon. He was secretly cremated.

On the 20th anniversary of John's death, a billboard in Times Square said '676,000 other people have been killed by guns in the United States since Lennon died'.

5.00pm   A Limousine arrives outside the Dakota apartment building to collect John and Yoko.

5.05pm   Fans see John and Yoko leave the Dakota building. A few fans ask for autographs. Mark Chapman is one of them.

5.25pm   John and Yoko arrive at the recording studio and begin to work on the new album.

10.30pm   They leave the recording studio to go home, have something to eat and to rest.

10.48pm   John and Yoko arrive back at the Dakota building.

10.50pm   Mark Chapman calls John's name. John turns. Chapman shoots John in the chest. John falls to the ground saying, 'I've been shot'.

10.51pm   Yoko Ono cradles John in her arms and begs for help.

10.52pm   A police car arrives. Chapman is arrested. John is taken in the car, but dies before he reaches hospital.

Bath Chronicle
Wednesday, 10th December, 1980

'MADMAN' GUNS DOWN JOHN THE BEATLE

John Lennon – one of his last pictures

JOHN LENNON was shot dead late last night as he returned to his New York home with his wife Yoko Ono.

The 40-year-old musician, the founder and driving force behind the legendary Beatles, was rushed to Roosevelt Hospital, but was dead on arrival.

Police said "a local screwball" with no apparent motive for shooting Lennon had been charged with murder.

He is 25-year-old Mark David Chapman, of Honolulu, Hawaii.

Chapman had got Lennon's autograph earlier in the evening as John and Yoko left their home in the Dakota, a luxury apartment block across from Central Park.

When the couple returned, Chapman emerged from around the corner of 72nd Street and began arguing with Lennon as he stepped out of his limousine.

Then, Senior Detective James Sullivan said, Chapman took up combat stance and emptied five shots into the singer's chest.

Lennon yelled, "I'm shot," staggered up a few steps into the building and collapsed.

Chapman made no attempt to escape and just threw the gun on the ground.

Yoko rode with Lennon to hospital, crying and shouting over and over again: "Tell me it isn't true."

Dr Stephan Lynn, of Roosevelt Hospital, said Lennon suffered multiple gunshot wounds in his chest, left arm and back.

He had no doubt that Lennon was "dead at the moment the first shots entered his body."

He added, "Extensive resuscitation efforts were made and despite transfusions and other methods he could not be revived."

Dr Lynn said that when he told Yoko of Lennon's death, "she was most distraught and found it hard to accept."

But she insisted on returning home to break the news to their five-year-old son, Sean.

Lennon, who married Yoko, 47, after a divorce from his wife, Cynthia, moved to New York after the break-up of the Beatles.

Each member of the group went his own way, Lennon living a hermit-like existence. He had described his life in recent years as that of a "house-husband" while Yoko handled their extensive business interests.

He also had a son, Julian 17, by his first marriage.

In one of his final interviews, Lennon was optimistic about the future after five years in semi-reclusion.

"You make your own dream. That's the Beatles story, isn't it? That's Yoko's story. That's what I'm saying now," Lennon said in an interview to be published in January.

"It's quite possible to do anything. There's nothing new under the sun."

At Bath record shops, there were differing reactions to Lennon's death.

Records Unlimited in Westgate Street has ordered the entire back catalogue of Lennon records and manager Mr Mike Wotton predicts particularly big business for the single 'Happy Christmas War is Over'.

"It may not seem very nice but it looks like the public demand is going to be there so we shall have to meet it," he said.

A spokesman for Wessex Records in The Corridor said he had sold four Lennon singles before 8.30 this morning. "We shall be stocking large quantities of all his records now."

But Mr Pete Dolan, manager of Music Market, in Burton Street, said, "There is no way we shall be cashing in on this tragedy. We shall not be getting extra supplies of his records or pushing them in any way. It is very sad."

A spokesman for Cruisin' Records, in John Street, agreed: "We always have a lot of Lennon records anyway, but we shall not be ordering more."

Writing
across the
Curriculum

The Times
Wednesday, 10th December, 1980

Violent end of 1960s hero evokes parallel with killing of Kennedy

Wave of grief over John Lennon's murder

From Michael Leapman
New York, Dec 9

Hundreds of mourners, chanting "All You Need is Love" and other songs of the Beatles, clustered today outside the Dakota apartment building in New York where John Lennon was shot dead last night.

Lennon, aged 40, was writer, singer and guitarist in the fabulously successful Liverpool singing group of the 1960s. He and Paul McCartney composed most of their hit songs.

Mark Chapman, a 25-year-old visitor to New York from Hawaii, was charged today with killing Lennon with a .38 revolver as the singer and his wife, the Japanese artist Yoko Ono, returned from a recording session just before 11 pm. Mr Chapman had been lurking round the building for days and earlier in the evening had asked Lennon for his autograph.

Lennon shouted, "I'm shot" and staggered into the building's entrance booth. He was driven to a hospital nearby in a police car, but was dead when he arrived.

"Tell me it isn't true," Miss Ono sobbed, as the news was broken to her. Mr Chapman made no attempt to flee.

When the doorman asked him whether he knew what he had done, he is alleged to have said: "I just shot John Lennon."

When Mr Chapman was formally charged this afternoon, Miss Kim Hogrefe, the assistant district attorney, said that he had borrowed money to come to New York specifically to kill Lennon. The Judge ordered him held without bail pending a psychiatric examination which his court-appointed lawyer had requested.

The lawyer said Mr Chapman had twice in the past attempted suicide and had been committed to mental institutions.

Miss Hogrefe said that Mr Chapman had $2,000 (about £800) in cash on him when he was arrested a few minutes after the shooting.

Police denied earlier reports that Mr Chapman had a record of arrests, including armed robbery.

Mr Chapman, who has lived in Hawaii for the last few years, grew up in Georgia. A police source suggested that his motive may have been dissatisfaction with the scribbled autograph Lennon had given him a few hours earlier, but this would not tally with Miss Hogrefe's allegation that the killing was planned in advance.

People who knew Mr Chapman in Georgia said that he had been an amateur guitarist. He became interested in religion at school and had worked since as a security guard.

An extraordinary upsurge of grief overwhelms America today. Scores of radio stations are playing non-stop recordings from the Beatles' heyday in the 1960s when they became, according to the Guinness Book of Records, the most successful recording group in history.

Sorrow over the loss of a prodigally talented musician is mixed with horror that, once again in America, an assassin has found it

Yoko Ono is supported by record producer David Geffen as she leaves the hospital where John Lennon was taken.

a matter of absurd simplicity to destroy a life at whim. In the immediate aftermath, the killing is being compared with the murder of President Kennedy in 1963, immediately prior to the Beatles' greatest success.

It may not be as unbalanced a comparison as it sounds. Both Lennon and Kennedy represented, in their different ways, the aspirations of a generation, which a quick squeeze of a trigger helped to destroy.

Tributes in the press and from people interviewed in the street are emphasizing how the Beatles became an integral part of the world Americans in **continued on page 7, col 3**

Chapter 2

Report writing

What is a report text?

A report is a non-chronological text written to describe or classify something. It brings together a set of related information and sorts it into paragraphs of closely connected facts. Reports can also be used to compare and contrast.

Structural features

- Usually begins with an introduction to orientate the reader. Tells us 'who', 'what', 'where' and 'when'

- Main body of text is organised into paragraphs describing particular aspects of the subject

- Ends with a conclusion that briefly summarises the text

- Non-chronological

Linguistic features

- Often written in the present tense (except for historical reports)

- Usually uses generic nouns and pronouns (such as people, cats, buildings) rather than specific ones

- Written in an impersonal third person style

- Factual writing often using technical words

- Language is used to describe and differentiate

- Linking words and phrases are used

- Occasional use of the passive

Examples of reports

- non-fiction books

- newspaper/magazine articles

- information leaflets, tourist guidebooks

Teaching report writing

Writing a non-chronological report is a bit like collecting shells on the beach in a bucket and then sorting them into piles of similar shells, discarding anything that is damaged or has been scooped up that isn't a shell!

Children need to learn to gather from research relevant information about the subject they are going to describe, sort the information into groups of facts that go together and then link them in a logical order, both within the paragraphs and between the paragraphs. They have to learn how to 'file' information into these paragraphs so that the reader can access the information easily and logically. Using subheadings for paragraphs can help children organise their information. They need to choose which information is most important to the reader and elaborate on it.

One of the difficulties for children is to be able to research the information they need without simply copying out (or printing out) passages from reference sources. They need to be taught how to select key words and phrases and use them in their own sentences.

Report writing – progression

Simple non-chronological reports are introduced in Key Stage 1 (Year 1, Term 2: T25; Year 2, Term 3: T21).

In Year 3 children locate information in books using the text structures – contents, index, headings, subheadings, page numbers and bibliographies. They record information from texts and write simple non-chronological reports for a known audience (Term 1: T17, T18, T21, T22).

In Year 4 children identify different types of text and different features of non-fiction texts in print and IT (Term 1: T16, T17) and they write non-chronological reports, including the use of organisational devices (Term 1: T21).

In Year 5 (Term 1: T26; Term 2: T22) children learn to make notes for different purposes and to plan, compose, edit and refine short non-chronological texts.

In **Year 6** (Term 1: T17; Term 3: T19, T22) children are moving onto writing non-chronological reports linked to other subjects. They review a range of text features and select the appropriate style and form to suit a specific purpose and audience.

Unit 1

Lesson focus

Science Unit 6B – Micro-organisms

Overall aim

To explore the features of non-chronological reports and to write a report about preventing tooth decay.

Science emphasis

This unit offers the children the opportunity to apply scientific understanding to their own personal health and well-being. By linking these ideas with research undertaken throughout the unit, the children will be synthesising everyday phenomena with known facts, which involves higher order thinking skills.

Literacy links

Year 6, Term 1: T13, T17

About this unit

This unit introduces the children to the idea of micro-organisms and how they can affect our health. They will learn to reflect upon their own dietary and oral hygiene behaviours. This will enable them to make a direct link between the cause and effect of tooth decay. They will be introduced to technical terms that will aid their approach to the rigours of writing scientifically. They will expand their vocabulary to include words that will provide a shared language for literacy lessons. The children will also discover an easy method for organising information into paragraphs.

Switching on

Learning objectives

■ To read and understand a non-chronological report.

■ To write a summary paragraph.

■ To learn that micro-organisms can cause tooth decay and that tooth decay can be prevented.

Resources

■ Sheets B and C (pages 34 and 35)

What to do

Tell the children that they are going to find out what causes tooth decay and how tooth decay can be prevented. Ask them about their own trips to the dentist. Discuss how they feel when they go, how often they go and what has happened when they are there. Ask them for their ideas on what causes tooth decay. Write these ideas on the board.

Tell the children that they are now going to read a text about tooth decay. Provide them with a copy of Sheet B or use an enlarged version. Share reading the report by asking children to read a paragraph each. Ask them to find

the parts mentioned in the report on the diagram. Ask them to give you a simple explanation of how tooth decay is caused, referring to the text and the diagram. Emphasise that micro-organisms are responsible for tooth decay.

Ask the children for their ideas on how tooth decay can be prevented. List these on the board. Hand out copies of Sheet C. Ask them to work in pairs and discuss what they, themselves, do and what they don't do. Get feedback from a few children on the differences between them and the Gleam Family. Point out that in the report, sugar and starch are mentioned as food for micro-organisms and that the Gleam family don't eat many snacks or buy sweet, sticky or very starchy food. Ask the children to suggest to you foods that are probably full of sugar or starch. List these on the board. Ask them to give you one example of a food they eat that might be just the meal ticket for micro-organisms in their mouths.

Tell the children that they are now going to write two lists. One list will be a list of food they will typically eat in one day. The other list is their typical daily tooth care.

Tell them to highlight anything in their daily diet that should be avoided and to add to their daily tooth care anything from the Gleam Family sheet they do not already do.

Give the children ten minutes to do this. When they have finished, ask them to tell you what they have decided should be avoided in order not to give the micro-organisms in their mouths food and to tell you what they have added to their dental care list.

Write on the board the following terms: micro-organisms, plaque, enamel, saliva, bacteria, acid, dissolves, cavities.

Ask them to use Sheets B and C and the terms on the board to explain to you orally why avoiding sweet and starchy food and having a good tooth care routine is helpful in preventing tooth decay.

Tell them that you would now like them to write two paragraphs – one to give scientific reasons why avoiding certain foods is helpful in preventing tooth decay, the other to give scientific reasons why good tooth care is helpful in preventing tooth decay. Tell them to use all the information provided and use the terms on the board. They could work in pairs for this task.

Plenary

Ask some of the children to read their 'scientific reasons' paragraphs to the rest of the class. Ensure that the children have understood the processes of micro-organisms on teeth and that they have used scientific language. Refer back to the report on Sheet B by reading out the last paragraph. Tell them that they are going to find out more about preventing tooth decay in order to write a report about it – this will help them and other children to avoid any unpleasant experiences with tooth decay!

Revving up

Learning Objective

■ To investigate the key features of non-chronological reports.

Resources

■ Sheets A and B (pages 33 and 34)

■ Coloured pencils

What to do

The children will need their own copies of Sheet B for this lesson. You will need an enlarged version of Sheet A (with the annotations covered up with sticky-notes).

Tell the children they are going to find out about the special features of a non-chronological report in order to be able to write their own later on. Remind them about the report they read on tooth decay (Sheet B). Tell them that this text was a non-chronological report. What do they think non-chronological means? Share ideas and then explain the meaning of the term. Ask them to tell you what they think a report is.

Now ask the children to look at their own copy of the report on tooth decay (Sheet B). Explain that reports usually have a title that tells the reader what the report is about. They then open with an introduction that explains in more detail what the report will contain. (Uncover the annotations for the features on the enlarged version as you go through the lesson.)

Explain that reports often use technical or scientific language. Ask the children to look through the report and suggest a few words or phrases they think are scientific. Explain that technical language is used to provide factual descriptions of what is being reported on. Ask them to look at the report again and underline, in one colour, any scientific or technical words or phrases they can find. Share their ideas.

Ask the children to tell you what they notice about the verbs in the text. Explain that reports are written in the present tense (except for historical reports). Ask them to underline in another colour the verbs in one paragraph.

Tell the children that non-chronological reports use 'generic' terms. Explain that these are words and phrases that 'club' people and things together, rather than naming specific people or things. Provide an example by pointing out that the term 'dentist' is used, rather than, for example, Mrs Smith the dentist. Ask them to find other generic terms and underline them in an alternative colour.

Go through the remaining features of the report, such as the use of paragraphs and a conclusion. Can they tell you what each paragraph is about? What do they notice about the conclusion?

Ask the children to mark on their own copies of the report the title, introduction and the conclusion in the appropriate places.

Plenary

Tell the children that you would like them to help you create a checklist for writing a report. What are the special features of non-chronological reports? Together, create a simple checklist that can be displayed in the classroom for future reference.

Taking off

Learning objective

■ To plan a non-chronological report.

Resources

■ Sheets B and C (pages 34 and 35)

■ Information books about caring for teeth

■ Sheets of A5 paper

What to do

Tell the children that they are now going to plan their non-chronological reports on preventing tooth decay.

Explain that in order to do this, you and they are going to share writing a title and an introduction. They are then going to organise the information for their reports into paragraphs.

Ask the children to suggest a straightforward title that will explain to the reader what the report is about (for example, 'Preventing tooth decay').

Ask them to refer to their copies of Sheet B and read the first two paragraphs again. Challenge someone to explain to you, in their own words, how tooth decay is caused. Now model writing the introduction. What follows is for your eyes only, to use or adapt as you wish. What you say is written in italics; what you write is written in bold.

> *I am going to model writing an introduction, so that you can see and hear what happens when I write. You are not allowed to help me at all at this point. Now, what do I need for the introduction of a non-chronological report? I need to tell the reader what the report is going to be about and answer the sort of questions that begin with 'who', 'what', 'where' and 'when.' This report is about preventing tooth decay. I have the title 'Preventing tooth decay' so what could I say now?*

There are many ways to prevent tooth decay.

That immediately tells the reader the answer to what this report is really about. It's not long enough for an introduction, so I shall put a little bit more in.

This includes cleaning teeth, keeping the mouth clean, special care for children and the elderly, visiting the dentist, protecting teeth and having a healthy diet.

For the rest of the report, I can use the above list as my paragraphs. I have used the present tense – 'includes', 'keeping'. I have used generic terms. Look, I have written 'children', not 'Joe' or 'Mary'. It's a good start.

When this is finished, reread it to the children and ask them if there are any alterations they would like to make. When everyone is happy with the passage, tell them to copy it down as their opening paragraph.

Provide each child or pair with five pieces of A5 paper. Explain that they are now going to organise their information into suitable paragraphs. Ask them to write each of the following headings on a different piece of paper: Cleaning teeth, Keeping the mouth clean, Children and elderly people, Visiting the dentist and protecting teeth, A healthy diet.

Explain that you want them to write notes from Sheets B and C (and any other resources you want to provide) under each of the headings on the pieces of paper. Remind them that they need to include information about why preventative methods are helpful to us.

Tell them that once they have done this they should put their pieces of paper together in a sequence that they think is suitable, beginning with the opening paragraph. (They could number their pieces of paper and put them together with paper clips.)

While they are doing this sit with a group of children and help them to sort the information under the different headings. Encourage them to use scientific language, the present tense and generic terms. Discuss with the children their choices for the order they put the pieces of paper in.

Plenary

Ask some children to give the class examples of what they have put under the different headings. Discuss with them if they think these children have organised the information correctly, so that it fits in with the heading. Ask some other children to give the class examples of

the order of their headings. Ask them to give you reasons for their choices and briefly evaluate these choices with the class.

Remind the children that a report usually ends with a conclusion. Ask them to remind you what their report is about. Agree some appropriate conclusions.

Flying solo

Learning objectives

■ To write a non-chronological report.

Resources

■ Sheet A (page 33)

■ Children's planning sheets from previous lesson

What to do

Tell the children that they are going to use their planning sheets from the previous lesson to write their report. Share an enlarged version of Sheet A to revise the main features of a non-chronological report.

Ask the children to go through their planning sheets to ensure they are happy with the information they have gathered and the order that it is in.

Remind them that they already have the title and the introduction from the shared writing session. Explain that they now need to refer to each piece of A5 paper, in sequence, and, using the linguistic features they have learned, write a paragraph for each piece of paper. Tell them that they can incorporate diagrams and pictures, but that these must be done after the writing.

Give the children plenty of time for writing their reports. It is important that during independent writing they are not disturbed by other children or adults – they need time to think, organise and write.

If there are any children who need support during this activity, take their first piece of A5 paper and ask them to verbalise to you how they think they should write the information it contains, using the linguistic features they have learned. If necessary, verbalise to them how they could write this paragraph, allow them to write it and then point out the linguistic features in what they have written. Suggest to them that they now tell you how to write the next paragraph and so on.

When they are ready to write the conclusion, remind them of the modelled writing for the introduction and the items discussed after this. Remind them that a conclusion briefly sums up the text. Ask them to write their conclusions and ask for examples to share and discuss when they have finished.

Plenary

Ask the children to look at the report checklist on display and to go through their reports, ticking off the features they have included. If they can't find any evidence, ask them to note at the bottom of their report what feature(s) they think is missing. Tell them that they can edit their work to include this feature later.

Ask a few children for examples of their conclusions. Discuss with them a good example of a conclusion.

Tooth decay

title
to say what the report is about

Tooth decay is the destruction of the enamel or outer surface of a tooth. Teeth are often coated in plaque, which is a white, sticky film. Plaque is made from proteins in saliva and sugary materials in the mouth. Bacteria grow in plaque and use the sugar and starch from food to produce acids, which eat away at the enamel of the tooth.

introduction to orientate the reader

generic term

Plaque bacteria, sugar and a weak tooth surface are present when tooth decay occurs. Many micro-organisms in the mouth can cause tooth decay, but the main bacteria is called Streptococcus mutans. This bacterium changes simple sugars into lactic acid. As this acid builds up, it dissolves minerals in the enamel. This causes holes called 'cavities'. If this is not treated, the hole gets deeper and deeper and spreads to the middle layer of the tooth, called the pulp, and inflammation occurs. It is this that causes toothache.

third person

non-chronological organisation

Dentists can diagnose tooth decay. Sometimes the patient will visit a dentist for a check up and is not aware of the problem. The dentist can see a dark spot or pit in the tooth. They will sometimes shine a light from behind the tooth to check for tooth decay. This is called 'transillumination'. If the tooth is decayed, shadows will appear when the light is shining on the tooth. A dentist will use X-rays to see how far the decay has gone. Another way of checking for tooth decay is to use a sharp instrument against the enamel of the tooth. A dentist can use a special dye that stains bits of a tooth that has lost part of its enamel. This is also useful to check that all decay has been removed before giving the patient a filling.

information organised in paragraphs

present tense

If the dentist finds some tooth decay, all the decay will be removed. The dentist will shape the sides of the cavity and fill the cavity with silver amalgam or some other suitable material. If the decay has reached the pulp, root canal treatment may be needed. This removes the decayed pulp. A 'crown' will be fitted to protect the tooth. If, however, the pulp has become infected, the patient will need to take a course of antibiotics to kill the bacteria before fitting the crown.

technical words

Eating and drinking things that bacteria love and not cleaning teeth regularly are the main causes of tooth decay. Dentists have ways of checking for tooth decay and will use specific treatments to cure it.

conclusion to sum up

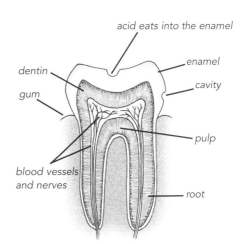

acid eats into the enamel

dentin

enamel

cavity

gum

pulp

blood vessels and nerves

root

diagram to aid understanding

Tooth decay

Tooth decay is the destruction of the enamel or outer surface of a tooth. Teeth are often coated in plaque, which is a white, sticky film. Plaque is made from proteins in saliva and sugary materials in the mouth. Bacteria grow in plaque and use the sugar and starch from food to produce acids, which eat away at the enamel of the tooth.

Plaque bacteria, sugar and a weak tooth surface are present when tooth decay occurs. Many micro-organisms in the mouth can cause tooth decay, but the main bacteria is called Streptococcus mutans. This bacterium changes simple sugars into lactic acid. As this acid builds up, it dissolves minerals in the enamel.

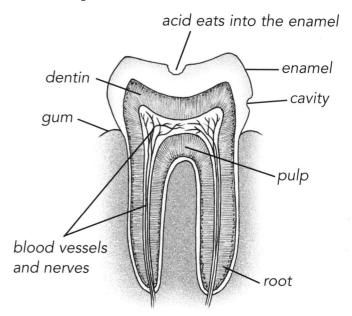

This causes holes called 'cavities'. If this is not treated, the hole gets deeper and deeper and spreads to the middle layer of the tooth, called the pulp, and inflammation occurs. It is this that causes toothache.

Dentists can diagnose tooth decay. Sometimes the patient will visit a dentist for a check up and is not aware of the problem. The dentist can see a dark spot or pit in the tooth. They will sometimes shine a light from behind the tooth to check for tooth decay. This is called 'transillumination'. If the tooth is decayed, shadows will appear when the light is shining on the tooth. A dentist will use X-rays to see how far the decay has gone. Another way of checking for tooth decay is to use a sharp instrument against the enamel of the tooth. A dentist can use a special dye that stains bits of a tooth that has lost part of its enamel. This is also useful to check that all decay has been removed before giving the patient a filling.

If the dentist finds some tooth decay, all the decay will be removed. The dentist will shape the sides of the cavity and fill the cavity with silver amalgam or some other suitable material. If the decay has reached the pulp, root canal treatment may be needed. This removes the decayed pulp. A 'crown' will be fitted to protect the tooth. If, however, the pulp has become infected, the patient will need to take a course of antibiotics to kill the bacteria before fitting the crown.

Eating and drinking things that bacteria love and not cleaning teeth regularly are the main causes of tooth decay. Dentists have ways of checking for tooth decay and will use specific treatments to cure it.

The Gleam Family

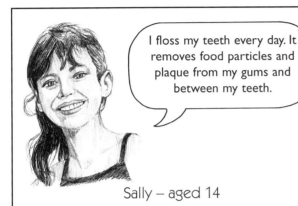

I floss my teeth every day. It removes food particles and plaque from my gums and between my teeth.

Sally – aged 14

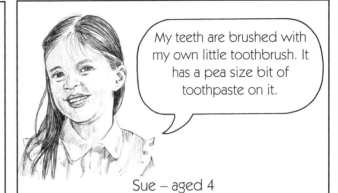

My teeth are brushed with my own little toothbrush. It has a pea size bit of toothpaste on it.

Sue – aged 4

I recommend using fluoride toothpaste because it slows down the destruction of tooth enamel. It can coat your teeth with a special sealant that will protect them.

Aunty May – the dentist

I make sure my family don't eat too many snacks. I don't buy sweet, sticky or very starchy food. I visit my dentist every six months for a check up and a proper clean.

Dad

I've got dentures, but I still keep my mouth clean or the bacteria in my mouth might give me gum disease.

Grandad

I brush my teeth after meals. I brush each tooth surface, the chewing surfaces on my back teeth and my tongue.

Emma – aged 9

I never fall asleep with a bottle in my mouth. I only drink milk and plain water. I never, ever, have a dummy that has been dipped in sweet things.

Baby Jo

I drink loads of water. I swish it round my mouth and swallow. It helps wash away bacteria and the food they feed on. I chew sugar free gum after meals. This creates saliva in my mouth which helps to keep it clean.

Tom – aged 16

Unit 2

Lesson focus

Geography Unit 15 – The mountain environment

Overall aim

To explore the features of non-chronological reports and to write a comparative report about mountain environments.

Geography emphasis

This unit encourages the children to explore the similarities and differences between different mountain environments in the world. They find out about mountain regions in Britain, Europe, Asia and South America in order to compare the physical features, climate, vegetation and industries that occur in each place.

Literacy links

Year 6, Term 1: T13, T17

About this unit

This unit encourages the children to develop their note making skills in order to write a comparative report. They learn about the key features of a non-chronological report and how to use the facts they have gathered in order to write paragraphs that contain comparative information. This unit could be carried out early on in Geography Unit 15 because it does not require any previous knowledge of the subject.

Switching on

Learning objectives

- To make notes.

- To investigate how mountain environments are similar and different.

Resources

- Sheet A (page 41)

- Atlases

What to do

Tell the children that they are going to learn about two different mountain environments – the Himalayas and the Alps. Have they heard of these places before? What do they already know about them? Write their ideas on the board.

Use atlases to locate the two regions. Ask the children to tell you how far away from Britain they think they are and how they might be able to travel there. Have any of the children been to these regions?

Share an enlarged version of Sheet A. Tell them that the text is a report that compares the two mountain regions. Read through the text, asking different children to read out different sections each. Discuss the meaning of any unfamiliar terms.

Ask the children to tell you what they can remember about the two regions after one read through. What is the same about them? What is different?

Tell them that you are going to show them how they can make notes about the two regions in order to compare them in more detail.

Provide the children with their own copy of Sheet A. They could work in pairs. Tell them that you would like half of the class to become 'experts' about the Himalayas and half to be 'experts' for the Alps. Divide the class accordingly and ask them to underline all the facts they can find about their region.

When they have completed this task, bring them together and draw a table on the board with a column for the Himalayas and a column for the Alps. Ask children from each group to provide you with facts for each region and write these into the columns on the chart. For example:

Himalayas	Alps
southern Asia	Europe
stretches over several countries	stretches over several countries
covers 2,400 sq km	covers 800 sq km
has high mountains	has high mountains
Mt Everest 8,848m	Mont Blanc 4,807m

Ask the children to look carefully at the chart and decide which things are similar in the regions (for example, they extend over several countries, contain high mountains, have extreme differences in temperature) and which things are different (for example, the Alps is a shorter chain of mountains than the Himalayas, the Alps do not have a monsoon season). Ask them to make two lists – things that are similar and things that are different. Again they could work in pairs for this task.

Share what they have found out. Why do they think the regions might have certain things that are similar? (For example, all mountain regions are high areas of land and will therefore have similar differences in climate and vegetation at different heights; the physical features of mountains encourage similar pursuits such as climbing and walking and hence create tourist interest.) Why do they think they might be different? (They are in different places in the world and will therefore have different geological and local influences.)

Plenary

Ask the children to tell you what they have learned about mountainous regions. How do they think the Himalayas and the Alps might be similar to and different from the mountainous regions in Britain? (Snowdonia, the Peak District, the Highlands of Scotland or the Mountains of Mourne in Northern Ireland.) Tell the children that over the next few lessons they will be learning about two other mountain areas in order to write a report comparing them.

Revving up

Learning objectives

■ To investigate the key features of non-chronological reports.

Resources

■ Sheet A (page 41)
■ Coloured pencils

What to do

Before the lesson make two copies of Sheet A and cut out the separate paragraphs.

Remind the children about the report they shared in the previous lesson. Tell them that they are going to learn about the special features of a report in order to be able to write their own later on.

Share an enlarged version of Sheet A. Remind the children that the text is a report. Ask them to tell you what they notice about how the report is set out. (Has a title and paragraphs). Why do they think a title is important? How would it help the reader when he or she is looking for information in a book, for example? (Annotate 'title' on Sheet A.)

Look at the paragraphing next. Ask them to tell you how paragraphs help the reader. Remind them that a paragraph is a section of text that has sentences all about the same topic grouped together. Tell them that in a report the first paragraph is usually an introduction and the last paragraph a conclusion. (Label these on Sheet A.)

Read out the first paragraph. What information does it contain? Explain that introductions in reports often tell us who, what, where, when and why. (Who/what? – mountain ranges, the Himalayas, the Alps; Where? – southern Asia, Europe; Why? – well-known ones.)

Tell them that the introduction gives the reader an overall idea of what the report is going to be about.

Read out the conclusion – what does this tell the reader? Explain how a conclusion briefly sums up the report.

Tell the children that you now want them to find out what the other paragraphs are about. Hand out the paragraphs (paragraphs 2 to 6) you have already cut out from Sheet A to groups of three or four children. Ask them to read the paragraph through and make a group decision about what the main thing their paragraph is about. Allow a few minutes for this and then share the results. Write a list of their summaries on the board, for example:

paragraph 2 – extent/areas covered

paragraph 3 – height

paragraph 4 – climate

paragraph 5 – vegetation

paragraph 6 – land use

Discuss why it is important to keep information all about one thing in the same paragraph. Ask them to tell you if it would matter what order the paragraphs were in (except for the introduction and conclusion). Explain the term non-chronological and compare a report text with a recount for example. (Write a label 'non-chronological' on the enlarged version of Sheet A.)

Discuss how the information about both places is interwoven into each paragraph so that the reader is able to find out about the similarities and differences between the two in order to compare them. Explain that this is why the report is called a comparative one – it compares the Himalayas with the Alps. Discuss how such a report might be useful. (It combines information about the two places in one report, rather than the reader having to read two separate reports and then compare the information himself or herself.)

Ask the groups to look at their paragraph again. (For those with the short paragraph about vegetation, you may like to give them the introduction and conclusion as well.) Ask them to read it through again and consider the following questions:

1. What tense are the verbs?
2. What special words are included in the paragraph? (technical/scientific)
3. Have words been used to describe things? (Are there adverbs and adjectives?)

Share what the children have found out and explain that reports are written in the present tense, contain technical language and use words to describe and differentiate. (Label examples of each of these on the enlarged copy of Sheet A.)

Plenary

Tell the children that you would like them to help you create a checklist for writing a comparative report. What are the special features that are used? Together, create a simple checklist that can be displayed in the classroom for future reference.

Taking off

Learning objectives

■ To make notes.

■ To plan a comparative report.

Resources

■ Sheet B (page 42)

■ Information books/sources about Snowdonia and The Andes

■ Report checklist from previous lesson

■ Atlases

What to do

Tell the children that in the next few lessons they are going to find out about two other mountain regions in order to write their own comparative report about them.

Write the words 'Snowdonia' and 'the Andes' on the board. Have the children heard of these regions? Do they know where they are? What do they already know about them?

Use atlases to locate the two regions. What can they suggest might be different about the two areas just by looking at their physical location? (For example, the Andes is in the southern hemisphere; Snowdonia is in the northern hemisphere – this will affect seasonal features; the Andes is a much longer chain of mountains.)

Share an enlarged version of Sheet B. Discuss the information contained on the sheet to make sure the children understand the content and technical terms used. Use the atlases again to find Mt Snowdon and Aconcagua and the seven South American countries that the Andes divides. Share ideas about what is similar about the two regions and what is different.

The information contained on Sheet B is sufficient to write a comparative report but if you want the children to find out more information about both places, allow extra time to do this. You could divide the class up into 'experts' groups where half the class find out about Snowdonia and the other half the Andes. Alternatively the groups could specialise in finding out about the vegetation of both areas, the climate, industries and location/physical features. Each group's findings will then need to be shared with the rest of the class.

Once all the facts have been gathered, tell the children that you now want them to organise what they have found out in order to plan their comparative report.

Remind them about the chart they compiled in 'Switching on'. Tell them that you want them to construct a similar chart for Snowdonia and the Andes. Allow them time to do this - they could work in pairs or small groups. Share their results. For example the chart could begin with:

Snowdonia	the Andes
Wales	South America
contained in one country	stretches over seven countries
area 2,171 sq km	length 7,250km
has low mountains	has high mountains
Snowdon 1,085m	Aconcagua 6,959m

Explain that you want their reports to contain at least seven paragraphs:

an introduction;

location;

physical features;

climate;

vegetation;

industries;

a conclusion.

List these on the board. Explain that you are going to help them write the introduction and conclusion in the next lesson and that you want them to concentrate on planning the other paragraphs first. One way of organising this is to tell the children to highlight information suitable for each paragraph in a different colour (such as red for location, blue for physical features, green for vegetation, orange for climate and yellow for industries). They can then go through their notes and the chart to highlight the different facts. Alternatively they could use five sheets of paper with the paragraph headings at the top and sort their information into each one.

While the children are sorting their information, work with a less able group, helping them to agree which pieces of information would belong in each paragraph.

Plenary

Share what the children have found out. What problems did they encounter when doing their sorting? Did they have difficulties deciding which paragraph the information belonged to? How did they decide which information to use and which to discard? Are they happy that they now have enough information to write their report?

Flying solo

Learning objectives

To write a comparative report.

Resources

■ Sheet A (page 41)

■ Children's planning from previous lesson

What to do

Tell the children that they are going to use their planning from the previous lesson to write their report.

Ask them to remind you about the key features of a report. Use the checklist from 'Revving up' to guide this discussion.

Share an enlarged version of Sheet A to remind them of the general layout. Remind them about the seven paragraphs they need to write (these could be written on the board) and explain that you are now going to show them how to write the introduction and first paragraph. Discuss ideas for a suitable title and then carry out the shared writing. The following is for your eyes only – to use and adapt as you think necessary. What you say is in italics, what you write is in bold.

My first paragraph needs to be an introduction to tell the reader what the report will be about. It needs to be quite simple. It needs to tell the reader what mountains are and which mountains are going to be mentioned in the report. I think I'll start with:

Mountains, which are areas of land higher than hills, are found all over the world. Mountainous regions have many things in common even though they may be thousands of miles apart like Snowdonia in Wales and the Andes in South America.

Now let me see, have I included information about who/what? and where? Have I written in the present

tense? Now my first paragraph is going to be about the location of the two places. I'm going to look at my notes to see what I want to include in this paragraph (look at a child's notes). I need to remember that this is a comparative report so I must make sure I compare the two places.

Snowdonia is located in Wales. It was established as a National Park in 1951 and covers an area of 2,171 square km. *Now I need to compare this with the Andes.* **The Andes, by comparison, is located in South America. It extends for 7,250km. It stretches over seven countries from Venezuela in the north through Colombia, Ecuador, Peru, Bolivia, Chile finally reaching Argentina in the south.**

Let me read that back to see if it makes sense. Am I still using the present tense? Have I included all the facts from my notes? No - I think I need to add something about the Andes being the longest mountain range in the world because this is a very important fact so I will make that sentence read:

It is the longest mountain range in the world and extends for 7,250km.

Ask the children to tell you if they think either paragraph could be improved in any way and make any suggested alterations. Then tell them to write the next four paragraphs about the physical features, climate, vegetation and industries. Remind them about using language to describe and differentiate. They could work in pairs to help each other.

If there is a group of children that need support during this activity, you could help them write group paragraphs with each child contributing a sentence each. Use Sheet A to give them suggestions for how the information in the paragraphs could be organised.

After about twenty minutes, bring the class together again to share ideas about how the conclusion could be written.

Plenary

Share some of the children's reports. Have they remembered to make comparisons in each paragraph to show the similarities and differences between the two places? They could work in pairs to help each other edit their reports in order to make improvements.

The Himalayas and the Alps

Mountains are areas of land that are higher than hills. Groups of mountains, called mountain ranges, are found all over the world. The Himalayas and the Alps are two well-known mountain regions in the world. The Himalayas are in southern Asia; the Alps are in Europe.

The Alps and the Himalayas have many things in common with each other. Both regions cover large areas and stretch over several different countries. The Himalayas extend from Afghanistan and Pakistan through India, Tibet, Nepal and Bhutan. The Alps form part of nine countries: France, Italy, Switzerland, Germany, Austria, Slovenia, Croatia, Bosnia and Hercegovina and Yugoslavia. The length of the Himalayas is, however, much longer than The Alps. The Himalayas cover 2,400km but the Alps only cover 800km.

Both mountain ranges contain high mountains, but the Himalayas has the highest of all. It contains Mount Everest, the world's highest mountain (8,848m) and 12 other peaks that are over 8,000m, including K2 (8,611m) – the world's second highest mountain, Kangchenjunga (8,585m) – the world's third highest mountain and Nanga Parbat (8,126m). The Alps' highest mountain is Mont Blanc which is only 4,807m high. The Alps does, however, include one of the world's most famous mountains, the Matterhorn (4,477m) which is famous for being very difficult to climb because it is a very steep-sided pyramid shape.

There are extreme differences in climate in both the Himalayas and the Alps. Like all mountain ranges, the valleys are warmer and drier than the higher slopes. The Himalayas have winter from October to February and summer from March to June. They also have a very wet monsoon season from June to September. At the base of the mountains the climate can be subtropical, changing to temperate at 2,130m to alpine at 3,660m. There is a line of permanent snow at 5,030m. The Alps have summer and winter at the same time of year but they do not have a monsoon season. The southern slopes of the Himalayas are the wettest whereas rainfall is higher on the northern slopes in the Alps.

The plants that grow on the slopes of the Himalayas and the Alps are quite similar. On the lower slopes forests of deciduous trees grow. Higher up there are conifers and between the tree line and the snow line, there are alpine meadows.

Tourism is a very important source of income in both regions and although this can be very beneficial to the people who live there, it can also have an environmental impact on the land itself

because of possible pollution and erosion. Both areas have farming, mining and manufacturing industries. Most people live on the lower slopes where the climate is mild and the soil more fertile.

It can be seen then that the Himalayas and the Alps have a great deal in common with each other and that their greatest differences are in the actual height and extent of the mountains themselves.

Snowdonia

What is it?	a National Park that covers an area of 2,171 sq km, Britain's third National Park to be established (in 1951)
Where is it?	Wales
Highest mountain	Snowdon (Yr Wyddfa) 1,085m, which is the highest peak in England and Wales
Climate	mild winters, cool summers. Rainfall throughout the year, temperatures range from 4° Celsius in January to 16° Celsius in July/August. No permanent snow line.
Vegetation (plants)	moors, bogs and meadows at low levels; deciduous then coniferous trees further up; alpines at the higher levels
Main industries	tourism, mining (especially slate), farming, forestry
Other information	population – 26,000

The Andes

What is it?	a mountain range that extends for 7,250km – the world's longest mountain range
Where is it?	South America – it extends through seven countries – Venezuela, Colombia, Ecuador, Peru, Bolivia, Chile and Argentina
Highest mountain	Aconcagua 6,959m
Climate	varies greatly – the north is rainy and warm, the central areas are dry with great extremes of temperature and the south is rainy and cool. Permanent snow line in the north is above 5000m but in the south it is above 900m
Vegetation (plants)	lower slopes – tropical rainforest in north; conifers in south
	upper slopes – highland meadows, grasses then alpines
Main industries	tourism, mining (gold, silver, copper, lead, iron ore), farming, forestry
Other information	contains some of the highest human settlements in the world

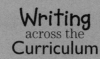

Chapter 3

Instruction writing

What is an instruction text?

Instructions tell someone how to do or make something. The success of the instructions can be judged by how easily the reader (or listener) can follow the procedure successfully.

Structural features

- Heading and subheadings
- List of items required
- Sequence of steps to be carried out in order
- Often has labelled diagrams

Linguistic features

- Usually written in the imperative mood
- Sentences begin with an imperative verb, 'you' or a time connective such as 'then', 'next', 'after that'
- Clear and concise – no unnecessary adjectives, adverbs or 'flowery' language

Examples of instruction texts

- recipes
- directions
- instructions for games
- technical manuals
- sewing or knitting patterns

Teaching instruction writing

One of the fundamental challenges of teaching children to write instructions is to help them consider purpose, audience and form. It is essential that they consider the prior knowledge and needs of their intended readers in order to write effective instructions that the readers can follow. Stress the importance of thinking yourself into the mind of the reader and anticipating their needs. As in writing poetry, children need to exercise some discipline in choosing just the right words and exercising economy of words so their sentences are generally simple with clear sequencing and precise language that can be easily understood by the reader. It is good to have readers using the instructions to test out the extent of the success of the writing.

While it is generally taught that instructions begin with an imperative verb, they can also begin with the word 'you' or a time connective. Children should be given freedom to judge which sort of sentence beginning is most appropriate. There is a good opportunity here to discuss the differences between the two different forms of instructional communication – speaking and listening and writing and reading – and the demands they make upon children.

Instruction writing – progression

Simple instructions are introduced in Key Stage 1. (Reception: T15; Year 1, Term 1: T13, T16; Year 2, Term 1: T13, T14, T15, T16, T17, T18).

In Year 3 children evaluate different types of instructional texts and are introduced to a range of organisational devices when writing instructions such as lists, bullet points and keys (Term 2: T12, T13, T14, T15, T16).

In Year 4 the key features of instructional texts are taught (Term 1: T22) and children learn to write instructions using linking phrases and organisational devices, such as subheadings and numbers (Term 1: T25, T26).

In Year 5 (Term 1: T22, T25) and **Year 6** (Term 3: T19, T22) children are moving onto writing and testing instructions, by revising the structure, organisational and presentational devices and language features of their instructions.

Unit 1

Lesson focus

Science Unit 6A – Interdependence and adaptation

Overall aim

To write instructions for growing plants.

Science emphasis

Aspects of this unit require that the children understand the dependency of plants upon certain soil conditions. The lessons provided incorporate the scientific requirements of knowledge and understanding of soil types and how plants depend on these together with concrete activities that appeal to children. These activities should produce results that can be observed by children and observation is a key aspect of scientific enquiry. Children often learn well when engaged in 'hands on' tasks as these produce an enthusiasm that may often be missing in more abstract situations.

Literacy links

Year 6, Term 3: T19, T22

About this unit

This unit will draw upon the children's prior knowledge of how to write instructions, which they have been rehearsing since Year 1. It is a revision unit, but incorporates other techniques which are useful for the children to learn. It emphasises the need for children to be writing for a purpose and gives ideas on how to provide this. The children will be organised into mixed ability groups which will give them practice in working cooperatively with each other. The children become experts in growing a particular plant type and share their knowledge with others. They will be asked to research their plant type and use this research to grow their plants. This provides the children with the opportunity to apply what they learn in a practical way.

Switching on

Learning objectives

■ To find out about the different types of soils needed for different plants.
■ To follow instructions.

Resources

■ Sheet B (page 51)
■ Gardening books or other sources that contain information about growing bog plants, rockery plants/ alpines, desert plants, indoor plants and grasses
■ Empty aquarium, watering can
■ Sand, rocks, heavy soil, compost
■ Basil seeds
■ Plants pots, saucers, broken crockery

What to do

Note: During this lesson, the children will be preparing areas in which to grow certain sorts of plants. If your school has an established garden and pond, then these activities will be straightforward. If your school has not yet established a garden or pool, all the areas described can be achieved in containers.

Prior to this lesson, it would be useful to ask parents/carers or friends of the school to provide you with gardening books, soil types, containers etc. The activities could be spread over a few sessions.

If appropriate or possible, tell the children they are going to organise a plant stall for the summer fayre (or similar event). Explain that they are going to be organised into 'expert' groups. Each group will undertake to become an expert in the following types of plants: bog plants, desert plants, rockeries/alpines, indoor plants and ornamental grasses.

Organise the children into five mixed ability groups and assign a plant type to each group. Tell them to collect the

gardening books/information that relates to their plant type. Ask them to find out the following things about their plant type:

What is special about these types of plants?

What is the ideal soil type needed to grow this type of plant?

What kind of aspect do they grow best in – shady, part shade or full sun?

How much watering do these plants need?

What time of year should they be planted?

Where in the world do these plants grow naturally?

The children could also make a list of names of plants in their group and draw sketches of them.

When the children have finished this, try a 'jigsaw' organisation so that all the children in the class can hear about each other's expertise. This can be done by asking a child from each table to go to another table and talk about their research findings. Each table should have children from each 'expert' group.

Gather the class together and tell the children that they are going to create some special places in order to grow the different plant types. Set the groups up with the following activities (this could be done during a science lesson):

Desert group: Make a mini-desert: Add some sand mixed with earth and place it in an old aquarium. Decorate the surface with stones and dead wood. Put the aquarium in a sunny spot. (At a later time, wearing gloves, these children can plant cacti. They will need to water them sparingly).

Bog group: Create a mini bog garden by using heavy, moist soil. This will need to be kept 'boggy' by plenty of watering. Place in a shady spot. (This group can later on plant some water loving plants.)

Grasses group: Prepare an area or large container with well drained fertile soil and place in a sunny site. (This group can later on plant some small ornamental grasses.)

Rockery group: Prepare either a small rockery by placing large stones in an attractive group or prepare a container with stones laid over ordinary well drained soil and place in a sunny spot. (This group can later on plant alpine plants.)

Indoor plant group: Prepare some pots with broken crockery in the base, fill with compost, water. (This group can later on plant a typical indoor plant.)

While the children are engaged in creating these areas, encourage one child at a time to visit the other areas so that they can compare the type of soils being used.

When the areas have been created, ask the children to describe the types of soil they have seen and felt.

Tell the children they are now going to read and follow some instructions for growing a plant from seed. Have they grown plants from seed before? What kinds of things have they grown and how have they cared for them?

Have prepared all the equipment as listed on Sheet B. Provide the children with their own copy of Sheet B and ask them to read through the instructions. Ask each group in turn to collect what they need in order to follow the instructions then allow them time to carry out the instructions.

Visit each group to ensure they are able to follow the instructions. If children are less able, share reading the instructions step by step, that is, read a bit, do a bit and so on.

Plenary

Ask the children if they managed to follow the instructions easily. Ask them what made the instructions easy to follow. Discuss any difficulties. Tell them that basil, sprinkled over tomatoes is delicious! Ask them to instruct you on how to write a simple recipe for this.

Revving up

Learning objectives

- To compare different types of instructions.
- To revise the key features of instruction texts.
- To make notes.

Resources

- Sheets A, B and C (pages 50–52)
- Gardening books or other sources that contain information about how to grow bog plants, rockery plants/alpines, desert plants, indoor plants and grasses
- Optional – a tape recording of the BBC radio programme 'Gardener's Question Time'

What to do

Provide the children with copies of Sheets B and C. Ask them to work in pairs and discuss the differences between them. Ask them to decide which instructions they would find most useful for growing the plants, the label-type instructions on Sheet C or the more detailed instructions on Sheet B. Ask them to give you reasons why.

Now ask them to consider Sheet B in more detail (it may be useful to use an enlarged version of the sheet). Ask the children to tell you any special features of instruction texts that they notice on Sheet B. Write these up on the board or annotate the enlarged version. Remind the children of any feature they have not mentioned and discuss its purpose, for example the use of numbering to aid sequencing. Use the annotated sheet (Sheet A) to guide this discussion.

Tell the children that at a later lesson, they will be writing their own instructions on how to grow a plant from their group (bog, rockery, desert, indoor or grasses). If appropriate, you could explain that they are going to do this in order to provide information for the customers at the plant stall during the summer fayre. Explain that their instructions need to be particularly useful for people who don't know how to grow particular plants.

Optional activity – Play the tape extract of 'Gardener's Question Time' and discuss it with the children. For example, ask them what sort of questions were asked, how the panel answered the questions and how much expertise the panel seemed to have. Point out to them that many of the answers were in the form of instructions.

Tell the children that you want them to find out about how to grow one particular variety or group of plants from their group type (for example, bog plants – iris; desert plants – cactus; indoor plants – cheese plant; grasses – bamboo and rockery – aubretia). Explain that this could help them to become an expert on 'Gardener's Question Time'!

Provide each group with information sources and ask them to organise how they are going to find and make notes about the information they need. They could work in pairs or the group could find out about different aspects each (for example, position, feeding, pruning, time of planting and harvesting, ideal soil type and so on).

As a result of this research you could stage your own class 'Gardener's Question Time' where each group take it in turns to become the panel where they answer questions about their particular plant, while the others ask the questions. (They could give themselves pretend names. For example, one member of the 'Gardener's Question Time' panel is called Fred Flowerdew – an apt name for a gardener!).

While the children are doing this task, assist those who need support with the research. Show them how to find information in a book and then ask them to tell you relevant information. Demonstrate note taking by orally transforming what they read into notes and then scribing for them.

Plenary

Share what the children found out. What problems did they have when doing their research? How did they record their notes? How did each group operate in order to help each other? Which sources did they find most useful and why?

Taking off

Learning objectives

■ To know how to write instructions.

Resources

■ Children's notes from 'Revving up'

■ Examples of plant labels

■ Card, scissors

What to do

Organise the class into their plant groups. Tell them that they are going to use their notes on growing their plants to write plant labels. Show them the examples of plant labels that you have and ask them to tell you what sort of information is on them. Point out that the information is in note form. Ask them why this is (because the labels are small and can only contain basic information). Point out that labels are often written in a very small font size so that more information can be fitted onto the label. Ask the children to estimate the size of the labels.

Tell the children that you are now going to model writing a plant label. Tell them that they are not to help you, but that you are going to show them how you would write a plant label and that they are going to listen in to what goes through your mind as you write. What follows is for your eyes only, to use or adapt as you wish. What you say is written in italics, what you write is written in bold. Following is the information you need:

Name of plant: Pieris Katsura.

Sold for its spectacular foliage colour, this stunning shrub has deep-purple glossy leaves which add colour to semi-shaded areas of the garden.

Height and spread: 1.5m (5ft).

Planting

1. **Keeping plant in pot, soak in a tub of water and then allow to drain.**

2. **In weed-free soil dig a hole twice the width of the pot and a little deeper.**

3. **Mix some general purpose compost or very well-rotted manure together with the lifted soil and put some of the mixture at the bottom of the hole.**

4. **Remove pot and place plant slightly below the top of the hole and refill with the mixture. Gently firm down to keep in place.**

5. **Water well and keep soil moist whilst your plant establishes its root system, this usually takes about a year.**

Tell the children that you are going to draw a large label on the flip chart, and fit your writing into it. Tell them this is not cheating, it has to be large so that everyone in the class can see it. Draw a large label shape on the flip chart.

I need to put the name of the plant. Labels often give a latin name. The plant I am writing about is called Pieris Katsura

Pieris Katsura

Now I need to tell the person who may buy this plant, why they should buy it. I need to put a short description of what it is like when it is fully grown.

This plant has wonderful foliage colour. Foliage means leaves.

It has deep-purple, glossy leaves.

Sometimes, labels put information under headings so that the reader can easily see how the information is organised – I shall put in some for my label.

Where to plant: semi-shaded areas of the garden.

Height and spread: 1.5m (5ft).

That immediately tells the reader whether or not it will suit their garden. If I was going to continue this I would now put in the next heading which would be 'Planting'.

Planting

Now I would put step by step instructions on how to plant this shrub when the person who buys it takes it home.

Ask the children to evaluate your label so far. How does it compare with the examples they have seen? Do any have a different sort of layout or organisational features? Discuss them. Give some labels to each child. Ask them to look closely at the labels. Ask them how the information is presented in note form, that is, what words are not used? (The definite article 'the' is often missing, commas are often used instead of connectives.)

Tell the children that they are now going to write labels for their plant types – they are to draw round the labels on paper and try to fit in all the information they should give inside these shapes.

Make sure the children have their notes from their earlier research, that they have plant labels to draw round and organise them so that they are sitting in their plant groups.

While they are doing this work, sit with a less able group and assist them by helping them decide on the information a buyer of a plant would need, finding this in their notes and cutting out any words that they do not need to use. Discuss with these children the ideas of different fonts for the headings for the information and how these devices enable easy reading.

When the children have finished their paper copies, ask a representative from each group to read out their labels. Discuss good points and direct children to revise any key omissions or delete any unnecessary words.

Now hand out the card and ask the children to cut out their paper copies, draw round them onto card, cut out the shape and in best writing, write their labels onto the card. Tell them to aim for a professional finish. On the reverse side of their labels, they can draw a picture of their plant type.

Plenary

Tell the children that in the next lesson they will be writing full instructions for growing their plant type. Tell them that practice makes perfect, but that they can now have some fun. Say that you are now going to share writing instructions for growing a 'fantasy' plant. Brainstorm, with the children, a fantasy plant. Encourage imaginative ideas, the stranger the plant, the more fun it will be. Now do a shared writing session on writing the instructions for growing this plant. This can be done rapidly and enthusiastically, but should contain all the elements of an instruction text.

Flying solo

Learning objective

■ To write own instruction text.

Resources

■ The children's own notes from 'Revving up'
■ Labels from 'Revving up'
■ Modelled writing from 'Taking off'

What to do

Children write best when they are writing for a purpose. If a summer fayre or plant sale is not appropriate in your circumstances and you have not yet provided a purpose for the children's writing so far, try now to think of one. This could simply be a class book on growing plants, or you could invite interested parents to view the plants grown by the children and provide leaflets for them.

Remind the children of the purpose for their writing. Orientate the children by having a discussion on the plants they have been growing, discussing successes and failures, how the plants might progress, the care they will need and so on. Remind them that they are the experts on their plant types.

Now tell the children that you expect them to provide full instructions for the planting, growth and care of their plants. Discuss all the features that are needed for an instruction text. Discuss what they think will be the best ways of laying out their instruction texts. Do they think, for example, that just writing it all down in one long passage will help someone who doesn't know the first thing about their plant? Remind them of the need to describe their plant before giving instructions on how to plant, grow and care for their plant. Explain that the labels they did in 'Taking off' need to be expanded to give a full account.

Tell the children that you will now show them how to do this. Retrieve the modelled writing you did in 'Taking off' and attach it to the whiteboard.

What follows is for your eyes only, to use or adapt as you wish. What you say is written in italics, what you write is written in bold.

Now, how am I going to expand on what I wrote for the label? The name can stay the same, but I might make it into a title.

Growing and caring for Pieris Katsura

Now, I began by giving a brief description of the plant. I can definitely add to that. I shall give the reader some information about the type of plant it is.

Pieris Katsura belongs to a group of plants beginning with the name 'Pieris'. These plants are evergreen and they all bear creamy-white little flowers in early spring. This particular Pieris has spectacular foliage colour, with deep-purple, glossy leaves.

You see, I have used some of the same words from my label, but I have given more information. The next thing I did was to use a heading to say where to plant it. I can do that again, but give more information.

Where to plant Pieris Katsura

Pieris Katsura likes a light, loamy soil with added peat. They prefer to be in a semi-shaded area of the garden. This could be in a place where they are sheltered from direct sun by other plants or where a light shadow falls upon them. They would not, however, like full shade.

Now, so far, I have expanded on the information I have given on the label. But, I have not yet used layout devices apart from headings to make it easy for the reader to follow instructions. I have also not used other features of an instruction text. I have not used a list of things that are needed. It is a good idea to leave a space for these and go back after I have written the instructions. That way, I can be sure of including all the things I mention in the instructions. I have not used imperative verbs or a sequence of steps. I could change the above paragraph to include these. But I must be sure to start at the beginning – and that is digging the hole for the plant. Let me try.

■ **Dig a hole big enough to contain the plant in weed free soil.**

■ **Make sure the soil where you will plant this shrub is light and loamy.**

I could add instructions here of how to do that.

Point to the above sentence and say *'I could add what I wrote on the label. Look,* (point to the text on the flip chart) *I could write* **To do this, mix some general purpose compost or very well rotted manure together and mix it into the soil.**

Ask the children to discuss what you have written. Make sure they understand that they need to use the information on the labels they did in the previous lesson and the notes they have made in their research. Ensure that they understand that they must organise their instructions in a sequential way.

Organise the children into their plant groups and ask them to begin writing their full instructions. Remind them that they can add small diagrams or pictures to illustrate their instructions, but at this point, they are to leave spaces for these and go back to them when the writing is finished.

Try to sit with another group than the one you sat with yesterday. If you have a teaching assistant, ask them to sit with your previous group and develop the work you did with them by helping them to expand their instructions. While you are sitting with your group, assist them in organising their information and discussing the sequence of the instructions.

When the children have finished their writing, let them share their writing with a partner in their plant group, comparing and evaluating each other's work. This work can then be word processed or copied out for best effect.

Plenary

Review the learning process with the children. Ask them to provide you with features of an instruction text. Ask them to explain how they managed to sequence their instructions properly. Ask them to give you a verbal list of what they have learned about writing instruction texts. Discuss any difficulties and successes. Ask them to tell you how writing an instruction text differs from writing, say, a story.

Ask them to think about how many things they have learned about writing an instruction text. Give them thinking time to do this. Share their ideas.

Sheet A

title
to tell
reader what
they are going to
grow

How to grow basil

picture
of end
product

You will need

list
of what is
needed

Light or sandy soil

Basil seeds

Flower pots and saucers or window ledge planters

Broken crockery

Water

What to do

present
tense

1. If you are using flower pots, put them on saucers.

sub-
headings to
guide the
reader

2. Put a few pieces of broken crockery into the bottom of your container to help drainage.

3. Add soil, up to about a centimetre from the top of the container.

4. Prepare soil by watering so that it is moist but not soggy.

numbers
to help
reader follow
correct
sequence

5. Place seeds 10cm apart and 1.5mm deep in the soil.

in
time order

6. Place container on a window sill in full sunlight.

7. Water early in the morning to avoid the plants from scorching.

8. Water every day but sparingly.

9. After 7–14 days the plant will germinate.

precise
language
without
'flowery' or
unnecessary
words

imperative
verb

10. When the plant is big enough to pick, pick a few leaves to use fresh or freeze.

time
connective

Figure 3

includes
explanatory
diagrams

How to grow basil

You will need

Light or sandy soil

Basil seeds

Flower pots and saucers or window ledge planters

Broken crockery

Water

What to do

1. If you are using flower pots, put them on saucers.

2. Put a few pieces of broken crockery into the bottom of your container to help drainage (Figure 1).

Figure 1

3. Add soil, up to about a centimetre from the top of the container (Figure 2).

4. Prepare soil by watering so that it is moist but not soggy (Figure 3).

5. Place seeds 10cm apart and 1.5mm deep in the container (Figure 4).

Figure 2

6. Place container on a window sill in full sunlight (Figure 5).

7. Water early in the morning to avoid the plants from scorching.

8. Water every day but sparingly.

Figure 3

9. After 7–14 days the plant will germinate.

10. When the plant is big enough to pick, pick a few leaves to use fresh or freeze.

Figure 5

Figure 4

Sheet C

Gunnera Manicata

ht – 2.5m

spread 3–4m

flowers from June – July

hardy

Planting instructions:

water thoroughly before planting

Cacti

use freely draining compost

provide maximum light

take care not to overwater in winter

Pampas

height 1.5m

hardy evergreen

free flowering

flowers August/Sept/ Oct/Nov

well drained fertile soil and sunny site

Lavender

an aromatic shrub with silver foliage

height 30–60cm

flowers from July onwards

any well drained soil

full sun

keep moist

Mother-in-Law's Tongue

tall foliage plant

thrives in good light

enjoys warm room temperature

water sparingly

Unit 2

Lesson focus

Design and Technology Unit 6A – Shelters

Overall aim

To write instructions for making a model shelter.

Design and Technology emphasis

In this unit children will build on their skills of designing and planning as well as marking out, cutting and joining materials. The children should have already investigated a range of shelters and identified which parts support and strengthen them.

Literacy links

Year 6, Term 3: T19, T22

About this unit

This unit builds on previous Design and Technology work done in Key Stage 2. The writing of instructions is explored in a very practical and motivating context which should grab children's attention. You will want to develop further specific design and technology skills, such as planning and handling of tools. Their understanding of written instructions will be consolidated and developed by considering the use of relevant diagrams as well as concise language suited to the needs of the audience.

Switching on

Learning objectives

- ■ To follow instructions.
- ■ To evaluate instructions.

Resources

- ■ A simple frame tent with its set of instructions for how to erect it
- ■ An adult helper

What to do

Tell the children that at the end of the term/month they will be making some special shelters in order to entertain visitors as part of their leaving celebrations (or whatever else is appropriate). Explain that they are going to design and make models of the shelters and write instructions on how to make the models.

Explain that in order for them to start thinking about the type of shelter they might create and how they might write their instructions, they are going to follow some instructions for putting up a tent.

Divide the class into manageable groups and arrange for each group to go outside (with an adult) at different times during the day to follow the instructions in order to erect the tent.

Before the groups attempt this task, make an enlarged version of the tent instructions and share it with the whole class. Point out any instruction devices used such as numbering, labelled diagrams, headings, subheadings, use of imperative verbs. Discuss with them how difficult/easy they think the text will be to follow. Can they anticipate any problems? Do they think there are any safety issues to consider?

Put the children into their groups and ask them to decide how they are going to organise themselves when it is their turn to erect the tent. Suggest that one person takes on the role of instructor and reads out the instructions. One or two children could be responsible for the equipment – they need to check that all the equipment is there before they start and make sure it is still all there when they pack the tent away ready for the next group.

Plenary

Discuss any difficulties the children had in following the instructions. Can they make any suggestions for improvements to the text? How would they rate the instructions on a scale of 1 to 10?

Revving up

Learning objectives

■ To revise the features of instruction texts.

Resources

■ Sheets A and B (pages 57 and 58)

What to do

Tell the children that they are going to look more closely at the special features of an instruction text. Show an enlarged version of Sheet B and ask the children to tell you how they know that they are looking at an instruction text rather than, say, a story. Note the features they suggest on the board with a blue marker. Because the children should be quite familiar with instruction texts by the time they reach Year 6 they should be able to identify most of the features. The features should include:

a clear heading/title;

a list of items needed;

easy to follow sequenced steps;

diagrams/pictures;

font and layout details for ease of reading;

imperative verbs;

present tense;

time connectives;

descriptions used for clarity rather than effect.

Using Sheet A as your guide, add to the list any features they haven't suggested. Write these in red.

Hand out a copy of Sheet B to every child and ask them to find and mark examples of all the features on the board on their copies. Tell them to use a different colour for each feature and to provide a key.

When they have finished this, gather them together again and ask different children for their responses. This is a good opportunity for differentiation in questioning as, say, the less able will be able to provide 'a clear heading' and the more able will be able to provide examples of imperative verbs or present tense.

Plenary

Ask the children to explain, in their own words, each step of the instructions on Sheet B. They can use the whiteboard to draw what they mean if they wish.

Tell them that they are now going to think about inventing their shelter. Explain that in the next few D&T lessons they are going to design and make the model of their shelter. Explain that you want them to make notes as they make the shelter in order to help them to write their instructions later.

Taking off

Learning objectives

■ To use notes to draft an instruction text.

Resources

■ Notes from D&T lesson about how to make model shelter

What to do

Tell the children that they are now going to write their instructions for making their model shelter using the notes they made as they were making it. Explain that first you are going to model writing instructions from someone's notes (borrow a volunteer's notes).

What follows is for your eyes only to use or adapt as you wish. What you say is written in italics, what you write is written in bold. Tell the children that at this point they are not expected to help you at all.

The first thing I need is a title that will make it clear what the instructions are for.

Making a Model Shelter

Now I need a list of the items that will be needed for making the model. I shall write each thing underneath each other.

Paper straws

How many do I need? Let me see if the notes tell me – ah yes, I need 12.

12 paper straws

What am I using for joining them? (refer to the notes)

Sellotape

What do I need for strengthening the joins?

Carry on like this until you have listed all the items. If the notes do not make it clear, point this out as you go.

Now I need to begin the sequence of instructions. I think I will use bullet points. I will check the notes to make sure I put the first thing to do first.

Measure the straws and cut them so that four are …cm long, four are …cms long and four are …m long.

Would a diagram be helpful here? Probably, and it is an easy diagram to do. I shall now draw the straws. I'll put them in a box and put a subheading under the box.

Cutting the straws

Have I used the present tense? Yes, I have put 'measure' not 'measured' which would be past tense. Have I used the imperative? Yes, I have made it clear that these are orders, not requests and I have not used any other language apart from the words needed to give the instructions.

Carry on writing out the instructions from the notes as far as you can. When you have finished, discuss with the children what could be done to the instructions to make them really clear.

Tell them that they are now going to write their own instructions in the same way using their own notes.

Work with a small group of children and help them write their instructions revisiting measurements or anything else they may have missed during the note making part. Remind them of the need for layout features and linguistic features if necessary, discussing with them how diagrams, font details and language can help make instructions clear.

Plenary

Ask the children to work in groups. Tell them to look at each person's instructions and decide, as a group, which one they think is the best. Tell them that they need to be prepared to explain to the others the reasons why they chose the one they did.

Share the selected instructions and reasons for selection.

You could take this further in a D&T lesson by giving the selected instructions from each group to a different group and ask them to make the model. They could then evaluate the instructions and make suggestions for improvement.

Flying solo

Learning objectives

■ To investigate different methods of presenting instructions.

■ To present their instruction texts in a chosen method.

Resources

■ A collection of different instructions that are presented in different ways

■ Children's draft instructions from 'Taking off'

What to do

Tell the children, that today, they will be investigating different methods of presenting instruction texts. They are then to choose a method and re-write their instructions for their model shelters in their chosen style.

Ask the children to think about how they learn best – by looking at pictures, by talking, by reading or by doing. Give them thinking time for this. Discuss their opinions. Explain that instructions can be presented in many different ways and ask them if they can think of any. For example, some instructions are given in the form of a series of pictures with text written at the bottom, rather like a cartoon strip. Some instructions use photographs, others just bulleted text.

Hand out the samples of instruction texts to the children. Tell them to look through them and take special notice of the following (write these on the board):

  headings, font types, diagrams, pictures, layout, presentational devices (for example, colour)

Ask them to decide what they particularly like about different instructions and make a note of these. Explain that they can choose aspects from a range of instruction texts that they think are particularly effective.

Give the children some time for this. Go round the class and point out any particular features you notice and discuss with the children their opinions on what they are seeing. Keep referring back to the structural and layout features.

At a suitable point, get feedback from the whole class on what they have found. Make a class list of the features they particularly like/think work best. Ask them to tell you what features they are going to use for their own instruction texts and to explain why.

Now hand out their instruction texts from 'Taking off'. Ask the children to use their investigation to help them re-write these instructions, using the features that they have chosen.

Sit with a group of less able children and help them focus on exactly what features they are going to use. Provide them with a step by step context for their writing. For example, say that the first thing they need to do is … then let them do it. Then say, the next thing you need to do is … and so on.

Plenary

Let the children show each other what they have done. Do this by asking each child to choose someone in the class to show their work to. Prompt a discussion between the children by asking them to find similarities and differences in the presentations of their texts. Then ask five children to come to the front of the class to show everyone else their presentation and to talk about the effects and how these enhance the instruction text.

Writing across the Curriculum

title to tell reader what they are going to make

How to Make a Camouflage Shelter

(By Amy Radcliffe, West Hoathly C of E Primary School)

list of what is needed – with exact measurements given

What you need

card for the base (23.5cm x 28.5cm) – any colour will do

5 wooden sticks (27cm in length)

2 pieces of card for the sides and roof (27cm x 30cm)

4 or 5 elastic bands

netting (52cm x 30cm)

green wool

paints – greens and browns

1 triangular piece of card (23.5cm base and 30 cm high)

1 piece of triangular netting (23.5cm base and 30 cm high)

sub-headings to guide the reader

What to do

present tense

1. Using scissors, make four holes in the corners of the card for the base.

2. Place four sticks into the holes, making sure they cross at the top.

3. Secure with masking tape.

4. Place the remaining stick across the top of the other sticks, then secure together with elastic bands until stable.

in time order

numbers to help reader follow correct sequence

5. Paint the other pieces of card in camouflage colours (greens/browns).

6. Cut out a square, 4cm by 4cm, on the triangular card and attach the triangular netting over the card.

7. Place the other pieces of card on the sides and back of the structure. Next, secure by rolling each end around the cross stick and hold with masking tape.

imperative verb

8. Decorate the netting with camouflage materials (for example, leaves). Now place this over the structure.

9. Thread a piece of wool through at either end of the netting and tie onto the sticks.

time connective

10. Thread wool through triangular netting and attach to sticks at the front of the structure.

11. Weave bits of wool through the rest of the netting to complete the camouflage effect.

includes explanatory diagrams

precise language without 'flowery' or unnecessary words

How to Make a Camouflage Shelter

(By Amy Radcliffe, West Hoathly C of E Primary School)

What you need

❑ card for the base (23.5cm x 28.5cm) – any colour will do

❑ 5 wooden sticks (27cm in length)

❑ 2 pieces of card for the sides and roof (27cm x 30cm)

❑ 4 or 5 elastic bands

❑ netting (52cm x 30cm)

❑ green wool

❑ paints – greens and browns

❑ 1 triangular piece of card (23.5cm base and 30 cm high)

❑ 1 piece of triangular netting (23.5cm base and 30 cm high)

What to do

1. Using scissors, make four holes in the corners of the card for the base.

2. Place four sticks into the holes, making sure they cross at the top (Figure 1).

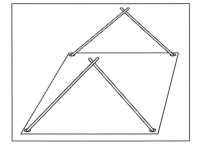

Figure 1

3. Secure with masking tape.

4. Place the remaining stick across the top of the other sticks, then secure together with elastic bands until stable (Figure 2).

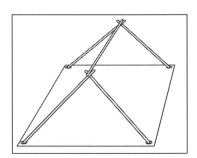

Figure 2

5. Paint the other pieces of card in camouflage colours (greens/browns).

6. Cut out a square, 4cm by 4cm, on the triangular card and attach the triangular netting over the card (Figure 3).

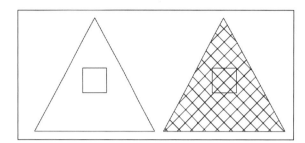

Figure 3

7. Place the other pieces of card on the sides and back of the structure. Next, secure by rolling each end around the cross stick and hold with masking tape (Figure 4).

8. Decorate the netting with camouflage materials (for example, leaves). Now place this over the structure.

9. Thread a piece of wool through at either end of the netting and tie onto the sticks.

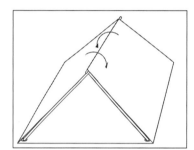

Figure 4

10. Thread wool through triangular netting and attach to sticks at the front of the structure (Figure 5).

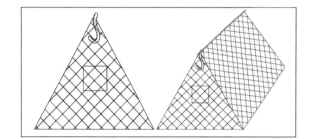

Figure 5

11. Weave bits of wool through the rest of the netting to complete the camouflage effect (Figure 6).

Figure 6

Chapter 4

Explanation writing

What is an explanation text?

An explanation tells us how something happens or why something happens.

. . . .

Structural features

- Title to tell the reader what the text will be about
- Usually has an opening statement to set the scene
- A series of logical steps explaining the process
- Often has diagrams

. . . .

Examples of explanation texts

- write-ups of science experiments
- encyclopaedia entries, text books, non-fiction books

Linguistic features

- Usually present tense (except in historical explanations)
- Third person (impersonal) style
- Uses causal connectives (such as 'because', 'in order to', 'as a result of', 'consequently', 'which means that') to show cause and effect
- Use of time or sequential connectives to aid chronological order (such as 'firstly', 'afterwards', 'meanwhile', 'subsequently' and 'finally')
- Often uses the passive
- Technical vocabulary
- Complex sentences

Teaching explanation writing

When children write explanations they have two main hurdles to leap. First, they have to be able to grasp the concept they are trying to explain, which requires some complex thinking skills, and then they have to articulate their understanding in the fairly rigid conventions of the written explanation genre. Plenty of opportunities to speak their explanation before writing will help children to organise their thoughts. Sharing their explanations with response partners at different stages during the writing process will give them a live audience to help them identify 'gaps' in their explanation and reveal specialised vocabulary that has not been clearly defined.

Making flow charts or simple diagrams helps to develop the children's own understanding of the process they are explaining as well as helping the reader understand the text more easily.

Explanation writing – progression

Children are introduced to explanations in Year 2 (Term 2: T17, T19, T20, T21) where they are required to read and make simple flow charts or diagrams that explain a process.

In Year 3 children develop their note taking skills (Term 1: T20, T21 and Term 2: T17) into making simple records including flow charts.

In Year 4 the children are introduced to the key structural and linguistic features of a range of explanation texts (Term 2: T20). They are also encouraged to improve the cohesion of their written explanations through the use of paragraphing, link phrases and organisational devices such as subheadings and numbering (Term 2: T24, T25).

In Year 5 children are required to read a range of explanatory texts, noting features of the genre (Term 2: T15), as well as planning and writing their own explanation texts (Term 2: T22).

In **Year 6** children read and write explanation texts, focusing on the use of impersonal formal language (Term 3: T15, T16).

Unit 1

Lesson focus

Religious Education Unit 6C – Why are sacred texts important?

Overall aim

To write an explanation of the Ten Commandments from the Bible.

Religious Education emphasis

In this unit children will be required to 'explain' a piece of sacred text – the Ten Commandments from the Bible. It encourages children to view the written word as a valuable tool in finding guidance for their lives.

Note – In this unit the children make their own interpretations of the texts. Sensitivity needs to be given to those children whose religious beliefs require them to accept the texts literally.

Literacy links

Year 6, Term 3: T15, T16

About this unit

This unit requires the children to reflect on the meaning of special books and to synthesise this idea with how the Bible has a spiritual meaning for those who follow its guidance. They will need to make inferences from texts and relate these inferences to their own and others' lives. The children will become familiar, if they are not already, with the archaic language of the Ten Commandments and transpose these into language suitable for younger readers. Through drama, the children will explore how the commandments came into being which will enable them to sequence and expand on events, tasks many children, even in Year 6, find difficult.

Switching on

Learning objectives

- To read and understand an explanation text.
- To listen and ask questions.
- To answer questions.
- To investigate why books can be special.

Resources

- Sheet B (page 67)
- A large box covered in gold (or special) paper containing a selection of books; for example, dictionary, manuals, a favourite storybook, special reference books plus a beautifully presented or decorated Bible
- School Bibles and the children's own special books

What to do

Show the children the large box – try to treat it as if it was very special. Ask them to try and guess what might be in this special box that you are treating with such care. Open the box and ask one of the children to take

out one of the books (but not the Bible at this stage). Whichever book is taken out, discuss with the children why the book is so special, what it can teach them, what you have learned from it, what life might be like if it had never been written and so on.

Have a special shelf ready in the classroom – this could be highly decorated or covered in gold wrapping paper. Ask a child to place the book on the shelf carefully. Repeat with the other books.

Explain that some books are particularly important to some people. Take out the Bible and show it to the children. Show them the decorations and any special features such as illuminated lettering.

Discuss why they think the Bible is important to some people. Explain that religious people such as monks used to copy the Bible out by hand and decorate it beautifully. Ask them if they would consider doing the same thing with their own favourite books. Place the illuminated/decorative Bible on the special shelf.

Share an enlarged version of Sheet B. Tell them that the text explains why the Bible is important to different people. Discuss the content of the text, sharing ideas about it. Were the children aware that different Christian groups used the Bible in different ways, for example? What do they think people have learned from reading the Bible? Discuss the meaning of the term 'sacred' and how this relates to the Bible. What sacred items do they know about from other religions?

Now tell the children you want them to think about a book that is special to them. Ask them to select their favourite book, and, working in a small group, show it to their group and explain why they like it so much and what they have learned from it. The others should ask questions about the book. At the end of this session, ask the group to choose one of the chosen books to place on the special shelf.

As the children are carrying out their group discussion, join in a group and listen carefully to what is said. Demonstrate, by your own behaviour, how to listen and ask questions.

Now hand out the school Bibles. Ask the children to find certain things in the Bibles, for example, the Old and New Testaments, Genesis and the parables. Discuss some parables with them, for example 'The Good Samaritan' or 'The Prodigal Son'. Ask them what these stories teach us.

Plenary

Ask the children what they have learned from the lesson. How can books be special to us? Why are some Bibles very ornate and decorative? What does this tell us about the value/importance of the book to those who read it?

Revving up

Learning objectives

■ To find out about the Ten Commandments.
■ To retell events in music and words.

Resources

■ Sheets C and D (pages 68 and 69)
■ Percussion/musical instruments

What to do

Explain to the children that they are going to write and give a talk about the Ten Commandments for younger children. Tell them that the written work will be an explanation text but that they also need to think of ways of demonstrating what they have written. Explain that they will need to know the Ten Commandments and be able to explain each one so that younger children will understand how these provide guidance.

Explain that today they are going to learn about how the Ten Commandments came into being and what these commandments are. The following activities could be done with the whole class together, alternatively, you could split up the story on Sheet C so that groups work on particular sections each.

Have ready a selection of musical instruments. Share an enlarged version of Sheets C and D. How much of this story did they know already? How important are the Ten Commandments to Christians? Why do they think they were set out for people to follow?

Tell the children that you want them to perform the story of Mount Sinai and the Ten Commandments to words and music. Ask them to think about how they could do this. Go through the musical instruments and

ask the children how they could be used to demonstrate different parts of the story. (A drum beat to count out the Commandments, a xylophone scale to illustrate going up and down the mountain, a crashing of cymbals to represent the smashing of the tablets, for example.)

Allow the children some time to discuss their ideas and then allow them to work in groups to complete the task. Go around each group, guiding their selection of instruments and the way they perform the words.

Have a 'performance' time. Let each group perform their words and music story to the rest of the class.

Plenary

Ask the children to tell you what they remember about the story of the Ten Commandments. How have the performances helped them to remember?

Taking off

Learning objectives

■ To understand the key features of an explanation text.
■ To write a planning frame for an explanation.

Resources

■ Sheets A, B and D (pages 66, 67 and 69)
■ Sheets of paper divided up into five large rectangles

What to do

Tell the children that today they will be making a planning frame that they can use for writing their explanation texts in the next lesson.

Show an enlarged version of Sheet B. Ask the children to remind you what the text is about. Tell them that it is an explanation text and that they are going to look at the special features of this type of writing in order to help them write their own explanation text in the next lesson.

Share an enlarged version of Sheet A. Explain that this version of the text illustrates some of the special writing features of explanations. Go through each feature to explain its meaning, making sure the children understand the terms. Tell the children that you want them to find further examples of some of these features in the text. Provide them with their own copies of Sheet B. Write the following terms on the board: present tense, technical language, time connective and causal connective. Explain that these are linguistic features of an explanation text and that 'linguistic' means the language used. Ask the children to underline examples of each term in a different colour each and create a key on the back of the sheet.

Share what they found out and then ask them to investigate the structural features of an explanation text. Explain that this means how the text is organised. Ask them to take each paragraph in turn and think about what it does and to decide on a heading for each paragraph.

While the children are doing this, sit with a lower ability group and lead the reading of Sheet B. Let a child read paragraph one and ask the group what this paragraph seems to do (tells the reader about the bible generally, so it 'sets the scene'). Let another child read the next paragraph and so on, asking the children what each paragraph is about and then using what they say to generate a heading for that paragraph.

Bring the class together again and discuss the headings that have been used. Point out how this explanation text has an opening that sets the scene and that the different details are organised into paragraphs.

Now tell the children that you are going to help them make a planning frame. Remind them that they will be writing an explanation text on the Ten Commandments for younger children. Draw five large rectangles on the board. Explain that each box represents a paragraph.

Ask the children what the title should be. Write down their response. Now, ask what the first paragraph of an explanation text should be about. Refer back to Sheet A if necessary. Remind them that the opening paragraph gives an overall, 'setting the scene' picture of the subject being explained.

Discuss what they think they could write in the first paragraph. Point out that they would need to explain, perhaps, where the Ten Commandments came from. Write in the top left hand corner of the first box 'Where the Ten Commandments came from'.

Now point out that there are four boxes still to complete and that the last one should be for their conclusion. Discuss what should be in the conclusion (a brief summary). Refer back to Sheet A if necessary. Write in the final box, in the top left hand corner, 'brief summary'.

Point out that the three boxes left need to be paragraphs about the Ten Commandments themselves. Ask the children for any ideas on how these paragraphs could be organised. If this is too difficult for them, suggest that, as their explanations are going to be for younger children, they could use the second box for explaining what the commandments are for. Write in the second box, in the top left hand corner 'what the commandments are for'. Explain that the last two boxes could be used to describe the commandments. Write in the third box in the top left hand corner, 'the first five commandments' and in the fourth box 'the last five commandments'.

Hand out the copies of the paper with the five rectangles drawn on it. Tell the children to use the headings that are on the board on their sheets of paper, placed in exactly the top left hand corner – they will need to leave space for planning their explanation texts.

Remind them, again, that they are writing for younger children and that this is an explanation text so their job is to explain. It will not be enough to just write down the commandments. They will need to explain, in simple terms, what these commandments mean. Provide the children with an example, such as 'You shall not bear false witness against your neighbour'. Tell them that this could be explained as 'It's better to tell the truth about people'. Go through some others, encouraging them to think about how they might explain the meaning of each commandment so that younger children will understand it. (You may want to define adultery as 'not being faithful to your husband or wife'.)

Ask the children to write their planning frames in note form – they can extend these during the next lesson.

While they are planning their frames, sit with some less able children and encourage them to use note form, rather than writing everything out in full. Demonstrate if necessary or you could create with them a composite

planning frame that can then be photocopied and shared by these children in the next lesson.

Plenary

Share some of the children's planning frames. Do they feel confident that they can now write an explanation? What things will they need to remember to include in the writing? (The structural and linguistic features.) Make a checklist and compare this with Sheet A.

Flying solo

Learning objectives

■ To write an explanation text for younger children.

Resources

■ Sheets A and D (pages 66 and 69)
■ Children's planning frames from 'Taking off'

What to do

Tell the children that today they are going to use their planning frames to write an explanation of the Ten Commandments for younger children.

Hand out their planning frames and copies of Sheet A. Give them a few minutes to familiarise themselves with what they wrote in the previous lesson.

Now tell them that you are going to model writing an introduction. What follows is for your eyes only to use or adapt as you wish. What you say is in italics, what you write is in bold.

First of all I need a title. I shall simply call it the Ten Commandments.

The Ten Commandments

Now, the first paragraph on our planning frame says 'Where the Ten Commandments came from'. So I need to do that. I can't use the present tense here because I am recalling what happened long ago, but I must remember for the rest of the text to use the present tense. I am writing for younger children, so I must keep my language simple. I shall write:

Long, long ago

I like that, it reminds me a bit of a fairy story – younger children will like that too. What next?

a man called Moses went up a mountain to talk to God. Moses was trying to save lots of people from being slaves and they had followed him to the bottom of the mountain. Moses needed God's help. While Moses was up the mountain, God gave him the Ten Commandments.

That is quite simple and 'sets the scene'. Now, I would like to help you write a paragraph showing the special linguistic features of an explanation text, so I shall start writing the next paragraph and point out the features as I use them. On our planning frame, the next paragraph says 'what the commandments are for'.

The Ten Commandments are God's way of telling us what rules we should follow in our lives.

I have begun to use the present tense. I have used the third person plural 'us'.

The commandments are written in a very old fashioned way because they were put into the English language a long time ago.

Now I have used a causal connective – because.

Ask the children how they think this paragraph could continue.

Now tell them to use their planning frames to write their own explanation texts. Remind them that the Ten Commandments seem very strict and cross and that they need to make them into friendly rules when explaining what they mean to younger children.

Go round the classroom while the children are doing this, assisting where you can. Try not to disturb them too much. Stop the class half way through this writing time to share any queries/problems they might have.

When the children have finished, arrange for them to quietly work with a response partner to read through what they have written, ensuring that structural and linguistic features can been seen in their writing. Also ask the response partners to check that the texts are suitable for younger readers.

Plenary

As the children have been concentrating and writing, change the mood of the classroom by asking them to work with their response partner in coming up with ideas on how their texts could be changed into a drama, a role play, a television show and so on.

After a while, ask for some suggestions from different pairs. They could be given the opportunity to carry some of their ideas out if you have the time.

Sheet A

general statement to set the scene before getting into detail

title telling the reader what the question is

Why is the Bible important?

The Bible is the most widely read book in the world. It is translated into thousands of different languages so that it can be read and studied freely by people who believe in its teachings. The Bible is often published as a rather ordinary looking book and can be bought freely from most bookshops. This is because the Bible is meant to be available for anyone and can be studied and read anywhere, although it is always treated with respect. In some churches, however, the Bible is beautifully bound and decorated and is treated with great reverence and care.

technical language

In a Christian Orthodox church, the priest will kiss the Bible before reading it and will carry it around the church so that the congregation will be able to bow to it. In Protestant and Catholic churches, the Bible is usually kept on a lectern. The vicar or priest will step up to the lectern during a service and read from the Bible and then explain the words they have read. In order to show respect for the words, the congregation will stand while the words from the Bible are read out.

causal connective

present tense

The Bible is divided into two main parts – The Old Testament and The New Testament. The Old Testament is a written account of oral story-telling from over a thousand years and relates histories and God's words from before the birth of Jesus. This part is called 'The Hebrew Bible' by Jewish people and they often refer to it as 'The Torah'. Every synagogue has a set of parchment scrolls with writing from the Torah. The Torah is written in Hebrew and Hebrew is learned by Orthodox Jews so that they can read from the scrolls. For Jewish people, these are their sacred books. They do not study or adhere to the teachings of The New Testament.

For Christians, however, the Bible incorporates The Old Testament and The New Testament. The New Testament was originally written in Greek and was mostly written within seventy years after the death of Christ. The Gospels, which are stories about the life and teachings of Jesus, are contained in The New Testament. It also contains the Acts of The Apostles, which records how the early church progressed after the death of Jesus. Although The Old Testament is used by Christians to guide their lives, The New Testament is the part of the Bible they most frequently refer to in order to understand what God requires of them in their everyday activities, beliefs and ceremonies.

complex sentence

The Bible is interpreted differently by different sections of the Christian faith. Some Christians interpret the Bible literally as they believe that its writings are absolutely the words of God given to the writers. Other Christians view the Bible as a collection of stories. They use the Bible to help them understand their faith and explore how the words can be relevant to their own spirituality and ways of life.

However and wherever the Bible is read, discussed and interpreted, it is the most important book in the world for Christians and as such it is a 'sacred' book.

brief conclusion to summarise

Why is the Bible important?

The Bible is the most widely read book in the world. It is translated into thousands of different languages so that it can be read and studied freely by people who believe in its teachings. The Bible is often published as a rather ordinary looking book and can be bought freely from most bookshops. This is because the Bible is meant to be available for anyone and can be studied and read anywhere, although it is always treated with respect. In some churches, however, the Bible is beautifully bound and decorated and is treated with great reverence and care.

In a Christian Orthodox church, the priest will kiss the Bible before reading it and will carry it around the church so that the congregation will be able to bow to it. In Protestant and Catholic churches, the Bible is usually kept on a lectern. The vicar or priest will step up to the lectern during a service and read from the Bible and then explain the words they have read. In order to show respect for the words, the congregation will stand while the words from the Bible are read out.

The Bible is divided into two main parts – The Old Testament and The New Testament. The Old Testament is a written account of oral story-telling from over a thousand years and relates histories and God's words from before the birth of Jesus. This part is called 'The Hebrew Bible' by Jewish people and they often refer to it as 'The Torah'. Every synagogue has a set of parchment scrolls with writing from the Torah. The Torah is written in Hebrew and Hebrew is learned by Orthodox Jews so that they can read from the scrolls. For Jewish people, these are their sacred books. They do not study or adhere to the teachings of The New Testament.

For Christians, however, the Bible incorporates The Old Testament and The New Testament. The New Testament was originally written in Greek and was mostly written within seventy years after the death of Christ. The Gospels, which are stories about the life and teachings of Jesus, are contained in The New Testament. It also contains the Acts of The Apostles, which records how the early church progressed after the death of Jesus. Although The Old Testament is used by Christians to guide their lives, The New Testament is the part of the Bible they most frequently refer to in order to understand what God requires of them in their everyday activities, beliefs and ceremonies.

The Bible is interpreted differently by different sections of the Christian faith. Some Christians interpret the Bible literally as they believe that its writings are absolutely the words of God given to the writers. Other Christians view the Bible as a collection of stories. They use the Bible to help them understand their faith and explore how the words can be relevant to their own spirituality and ways of life.

However and wherever the Bible is read, discussed and interpreted, it is the most important book in the world for Christians and as such it is a 'sacred' book.

MOUNT SINAI

1. After travelling for many months, the Israelites came to Mount Sinai and rested.

2. Moses climbed up the mountain to meet God. He was afraid.

3. God, in a mighty voice, said, 'Tell your followers that I have saved you all. When I come back, you must listen to my voice and keep the agreement I will make with you. If you obey me I will be your God and protect you.'

4. On the third day, God descended upon the mountain. Thunder roared and lightning flashed across the sky. A vast cloud descended and the sound of trumpets rang out. The people were afraid.

5. Moses went back up the mountain and met God. God gave Moses the Ten Commandments written on two slabs of stone. It was a very solemn and serious meeting.

6. While they waited for Moses, the people built a golden statue of a calf and they worshipped it with music and song.

7. When Moses came down the mountain and saw what the people were doing, he was so angry he smashed the tablets on the ground and broke them. He smashed up the golden calf.

8. The people went mad and rioted. Moses called on those who wanted to be faithful to God. Many came and they killed the ones who didn't want to follow the Ten Commandments.

9. When it was quiet, Moses went back up the mountain and God gave him new tablets of stone with the commandments upon them. There were the sounds of harps and angels singing.

10. Moses came down the mountain looking so radiant and wonderful that no one could look at him unless they covered their face with cloth.

Moses read the Commandments to the people and there was great rejoicing.

THE TEN COMMANDMENTS

1. *You shall have no other gods but me.*

2. *You shall not make a carved image or any likeness of any creature and bow down and worship it.*

3. *You shall not utter the name of the Lord your God to misuse it.*

4. *Observe the Sabbath day and keep it holy. You shall do no work on that day.*

5. *Honour your father and your mother.*

6. *You shall not kill.*

7. *You shall not commit adultery.*

8. *You shall not steal.*

9. *You shall not bear false witness against your neighbour.*

10. *You shall not covet anything that belongs to your neighbour.*

Unit 2

Lesson focus

Science Unit 6F – How we see things

Overall aim

To write an explanation of how light reflects off a mirror.

Science emphasis

This unit develops children's ability to explain their observations about light. By writing an explanation the children will have to understand the scientific rules that govern the behaviour of light and be able to formulate these into logical cause and effect rationale. This will provide them with the opportunity to clarify and organise their thoughts, observations and information.

Literacy links

Year 6, Term 3: T15

About this unit

The children will be exploring how light behaves through stories, experimenting and fact sheets. They will be turning parts of a story into a drama which will demand a high level of comprehension from the children. Through comparing different sorts of text, the children will need to be able to look very closely at these texts to define how each text 'works'. They will learn a new way of organising the information they have gathered. By explaining this information, the children will need to think logically and precisely so that they can clearly inform the reader of their texts.

Switching on

Learning objectives

■ To explore how light behaves with mirrors.
■ To revise what an explanation text is.

Resources

■ Sheet A (pages 75 and 76)
■ Torches
■ Mirrors
■ Boxes - cereal boxes or shoe boxes
■ A large card with the following 'magic spell' written on it:
   YDEPZEBEJDROWCIGAMEHTYAS

What to do

Before this lesson: This activity needs to be done in the school hall, with some prior preparation from you. Put the card with the 'magic spell' on a wall of the hall. Place boxes in various positions around the hall – one for each group of children. If you wish, put sweets inside the boxes to represent jewels.

Tell the children that you are going to give them a story to read. Hand out the copies of Sheet A. Allow them time to read the story through once – or read it to them. Briefly discuss the story. Tell them that at this point you do not want to know the answer to the questions at the end. Did they enjoy it? Have they ever used torches and/or mirrors to send messages or do tricks with lights?

Ask them to find examples in the text where torches and mirrors are used. When someone has found an example, give a child a torch and a mirror and ask the child to show you what the character in the story did. Ask the child to point out to the class where he or she thinks the direction of the light goes each time.

Tell the children that they are now going to enact parts of the story. Take them to the hall. Tell them that they are going to work in threes – two to be the children in the story, the other to take the part of the other characters. The ghost's head on the ceiling must be left to their imagination! Tell them that there is one box per group.

This activity would be enhanced if the school hall can be dimmed by drawing blinds, but a cloudy or rainy afternoon will do. Hand out the torches and mirrors.

Allow them a little time to 'play' with the torches and mirrors while they are seated on the hall floor.

Safety issue: Tell the children not to shine or direct the torch or mirror into anyone's eyes.

Then ask them to switch off the torches and put their torches and mirrors down. Tell them that they now have a couple of minutes to work out between them who is going to do what and where they are going to start. When the children are ready, tell them to start acting out the activities in the story.

Allow them ten minutes at the most. Stop them and switch on the hall lights. Ask different groups what they have managed to do and ask them to explain to the rest of the class the direction of the light as it travelled from torch to object to mirror to eyes. Ask them to answer the questions at the end of the story and to explain the 'backwards' writing and how to use a mirror to read it.

Tell the children that they have a little while to think of other things to do with the mirror and torch to act out in the story. If they are stuck, ask them questions such as *'Could you light the way for someone without them knowing where you are?', 'Can you find out what is inside the box without anyone else seeing?', 'How many times can you bounce a light from mirror to mirror?', 'Could you find something else that is round a corner or on top of a high shelf?'*

Give them five or ten more minutes to experiment with these ideas.

Plenary

Ask the children to explain orally what they observed. Insist that they begin with 'the light travels from the source' and encourage scientific language. Ensure that the children understand that the light travels in a straight line, is reflected at angles from the mirror and enters the eye.

Briefly revise what an explanation is – don't go into the structural and linguistic features of an explanation text at this stage. Is Sheet A an explanation? What does an explanation do? Tell the children that in the next few lessons they are going to learn more about explanations in order to write their own explanation about light and mirrors.

It would be beneficial for the children to investigate light and mirrors further in their Science lessons before the next sessions in this unit.

Revving up

Learning objectives

■ To understand the key features of an explanation text.

Resources

■ Sheets B, C and D (pages 77–79)

What to do

Remind the children that they are going to write an explanation text about mirrors and light. Tell them that in order to do this they must know how an explanation text is written. Explain that you are going to show them how to write one.

Tell them that you are going to write the first paragraph of an explanation that explains how shadows are formed. Explain that you are going to write a really bad explanation to see if they can work out how it could be improved. Use a flip chart or some other way of writing so that it can be kept. The following is for your eyes only to be used or adapted as you wish. The children are not allowed to help you at this stage. What you say is written in italics, what you write is written in bold.

I shall need a title. I am going to explain how shadows are formed. A really bad explanation will probably have a title that doesn't tell the reader what the explanation is going to be about so…

A Cloudy Day

That sounds more like a story. Well, I'll continue with my really bad explanation.

I have seen a shadow of the tree in the playground. It was darker than the rest of the playground. I like making shadows with my fingers too. Tomorrow, if it is sunny, I shall try drawing

round a shadow of Mrs Jones. I could always use a torch if it's not sunny.

Ask the children to think about what is wrong with this explanation so far but explain that you don't want them to tell you yet – they are going to read another explanation first that might help them decide.

Share an enlarged version of Sheet C. Read it to them and discuss the meaning of any unfamiliar terms. Ask them to read it through again themselves and make a list of any features in the text that they think shows it is an explanation. They could work in pairs for this task.

After a few minutes ask the children to tell you what they have found. Annotate the sheet with their ideas and add any other features they have not thought of, using Sheet B as your guide.

Now refer back to your poor explanation text about how shadows are formed and ask the children to help you improve it. Check that they are incorporating some of the key features discussed.

Now tell them that they have a real challenge! Provide them with a copy of Sheet D (and their own copy of Sheet C if you wish) and ask them to use the information in the text to label the diagram of the eye correctly. Ask them to tell you how important they think it would be to include a labelled diagram with this text. How would it help the reader?

Plenary

Ask two able children to show the class a situation they would normally have to explain, for example, 'How an ice-cream came to be on the head of a Year Three child'. One is to verbalise the explanation in a formal manner, using the present tense, generic terms and other linguistic features of an explanation text while the other is to demonstrate the action. Challenge the others to think of their own situation to demonstrate.

Taking off

Learning objectives

■ To plan an explanation.

Resources

■ Sheet E (page 80)

What to do

Tell the children that today they are going to plan their explanation texts. (They could work in pairs.) Inform them who their audience is going to be (a younger class, for example). Remind them that their explanations are going to be scientific and will explain how light behaves when used with a mirror.

Ask them to tell you any words they think might be useful to them when writing their explanation. Brainstorm a word list; for example: reflective, direction, angles, bounce, surfaces, ray of light, light source – and write the list where the children can have access and add to it.

Ask them to remind you of the many things that can be done with mirrors and torches and how light behaves. These could include: making light travel with a mirror, how to see behind you, how to see round a corner, how to see what's on top of a high shelf, sending signals and reading messages in mirrors. Tell the children you want them to incorporate as many ideas as possible in their explanations.

Explain that their first task is to create a flow chart. Tell them that they will use the flow chart in the next lesson to write their explanation texts. Tell them that the flow chart will help them to organise their writing and help ensure their structure is logical. Hand out copies of Sheet E and explain that they can also use this to help them.

Demonstrate the beginning of making a flow chart by using the example below as a guide:

How light reflects off a mirror

Light comes from a source (such as a torch).

↓

The light travels in a straight line.

↓

The light hits the mirror, which is a smooth, reflective surface.

↙ ↘

If the light hits the mirror straight on, it bounces back in exactly the same direction.

If the light hits the mirror at an angle, it bounces back at the same angle but on the opposite side of the original line of direction.

↓

The light bounces from the mirror and shines on the next opaque material it meets.

↙ ↘

Some light is absorbed by the opaque material.

If the opaque material is rough, the rest of the light scatters in all directions.

While the children are creating their own flow charts, walk around the class helping them. Stop the class from time to time to point out a good example or to discuss how a section of the chart could be swapped or put in a different place in order to make the sequence more logical.

When they have completed their charts, ask them to think about how they might show or demonstrate the phenomena they will be explaining. Discuss the possibilities. For example, they may wish to use large paper and draw labelled diagrams or use strips of paper or string to show the path of light. Ask the children to plan and prepare their diagrams and demonstration tools.

Plenary

Share some of the flow charts and ideas for diagrams or demonstrations. Discuss how well these work and if any improvements could be made. Ask them to think of anything they know that use mirrors to reflect light (for example, kaleidoscopes and periscopes) so that their explanations can include examples of how the science can be applied.

Flying solo

Learning objectives

■ To write an explanation.

■ To use a visual resource to support the explanation.

Resources

■ List of features of explanation texts from 'Revving up'

■ Children's flow charts from 'Taking off'

What to do

Prior to this lesson, select a good example of a flow chart and one that can be improved. Ask the children's permission to use them in the lesson.

Tell the children that they will be writing their explanation texts today. Ask them to read through their flow charts. After a few minutes, explain that you are going to help them make sure their flow charts are good enough to help them write their explanation. Share an enlarged version of the child's(or pair's) chart that needs improving and point out why it needs improving. Ask the whole class to help improve the chart. Share an enlarged version of a 'good' chart and explain why you think it will help the writer. Give the children a few minutes to amend their own charts as a result of this discussion.

Now return to the flip chart with the list of key features of an explanation text. Briefly revise the points.

Tell the children that you are now going to model some writing to show them how to use their flow charts and the list of features to begin writing their explanation. What follows is for your eyes only to use or adapt as you wish. What you say is written in italics, what you write is in bold.

I'll pretend that I have already put the title. Now, the first thing on my flow chart is 'Light comes from a source (such as a torch). I will need to expand on that, a flow chart is, after all, just notes put in the right order. What features do I need? present tense, third person, causal and time connectives and generic terms. Let's see if I can use any of these.

Light comes from several different sources, such as the Sun, electric lamps (bulbs), flourescent tubes and candles.

I have used the present tense and the third person. Now what can I say?

People sometimes make the mistake of thinking that when they see an object the light on that object has come from their eyes. This is not true because the light always travels from a light source to the object before we see it.

In this second paragraph I have used a generic term – 'people' – and a causal connective – 'because'. Now I can move on to the next step of my flow chart. It says 'The light travels in a straight line.'

When the light travels from a light source it always travels in a straight line. Light cannot travel round corners or up and down without something to redirect this straight line.

Now I have used a time connective – when.

Ask the children to discuss what you have written and discuss any alterations or additions they think necessary.

The children can then work in pairs, turning their flow charts into an explanation text. Move from pair to pair. Stop the class from time to time to remind them of the need for present tense, complex sentences, generic terms and so on. Read out examples that you find.

When the children have finished writing their explanation texts, ask them to pass them onto another pair to see if they agree that they have written a satisfactory explanation text. When they have been given approval, the children can begin to rehearse the explanation they will give to the chosen audience.

Plenary

Ask the children what they have learned from the lessons (about light and about explanations). If they were to produce a help sheet for Year 5 on how to write a good explanation, what would they include on it? Agree a list.

Give the children the opportunity to rehearse and then give their explanation to the chosen audience.

Mirrors, Torches – and the Case of the Missing Jewels

Bradley and Francesca stood outside the massive oak doors that led to the great hall of the haunted Castle Gloom. Outside, lightning cracked across the turrets and rain thundered against the gothic windows. Thieves had stolen priceless jewels and the two children had followed them into the castle. They had seen the thieves enter the great hall and close the mighty doors behind them.

"Listen, Bradley," Francesca whispered, "when we go in they will hear the doors creak. They don't know we're just children so they will switch off all the lights and try and hide. We've got torches and mirrors. We've got to find the jewels and get out without being caught."

"There's probably ghosts as well," Bradley hissed. "OK, on the count of three, we'll open the doors and go in. One-two-three."

The children pushed the doors which shuddered and creaked. They slipped through the doors which banged shut behind them, sending echoes through the hall. Lights were immediately switched off. Bradley went to the left and Francesca went right.

Bradley could only just make out huge dark shapes of furniture as he crept along the wall. The hairs on the back of his neck stood up. Someone was behind him! He froze. He held up a mirror and shone his torch over his shoulder. A terrible face appeared in the mirror. Bradley quickly switched off his torch and crawled under a chair.

"Who's there?" said a rough voice. "Where have you gone?"

Bradley shone his torch into the mirror so that the light seemed to come from across the hall. He heard the thief, who finally stumbled over a footstool, cursing. Bradley switched off his torch.

Meanwhile, Francesca had hidden behind curtains that covered an alcove. Before she had found her hiding place, she had noticed the outline of a man standing still, holding something. She held a mirror in one hand and carefully put her arm out through a crack in the curtains. She quickly thrust her other hand out and flashed her torch at the man, then switched it off so he wouldn't have a chance to see where the light had come from.

However, in that short time, Francesca had seen in the mirror that he was holding the box of jewels! Francesca decided to send a signal to Bradley. If she just flashed the torch, the thieves would know where she was. She held the mirror out again and tipped it so when she shone the torch at it, the light would reflect on the ceiling. From behind the curtains, she flashed the torch three times onto the mirror. As she flashed, the head of a ghost that was floating on the ceiling was lit up. A long moan ran through the hall.

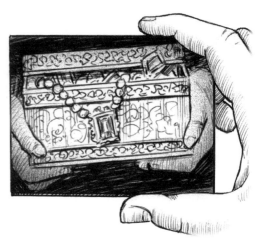

"My head! There's my head!" wailed the ghost.

The thief holding the box of jewels screamed, dropped the box and ran out of the hall. Francesca nearly followed him as someone slipped into the alcove behind the curtains.

"It's OK – it's me," whispered Bradley.

The children carefully crept out of the alcove and felt their way to the fallen box of jewels and picked it up.

"How are we going to get out of here?" Bradley murmured.

"I've noticed what could be a magic spell written on that wall over there, but if we go closer we may bump into the other thief and the ghost," Francesca whispered. "If I shine a light on it, it will be reflected in my mirror."

Francesca shone her light on the words on the wall and read what was reflected in her mirror. It said:

YDEPZEBEJDROWCIGAMEHTYAS

"What on earth does it say?" Bradley hissed.

"I haven't got a clue!" snapped Francesca.

How will the children be able to read the words the right way round?

Can you think of any other ways the children could use their torches and mirrors to help them in the story?

HOW OUR EYES WORK

opening paragraph to introduce topic

Sight is the most highly developed sense in humans. Eyes are receptors to light reflected from objects and the brain interprets these reflections into objects that we recognise. The eye itself does not produce any light and so without light we would not be able to see. Light sources can be primary, that is, they give out light directly, for example, the sun or a torch or secondary, that is, they reflect light from a primary source, for example, mirrors.

title to introduce what is to be explained

The eye is like a small round ball that sits in the *eye socket*. It is protected by the *conjunctiva, eyelashes, eyelids* and *tear ducts*. The conjunctiva is a thin protective membrane that covers the front of the eyeball and lines the eyelids. Eyelashes stop particles of dust entering the eye. The eyelids are closed frequently by blinking. This action maintains a moist film over the eye that enables it to move freely and also protects the main parts from dust. Tear ducts produce a salty liquid that acts as a cleansing agent for the eye. When humans cry, an excess of this liquid is produced so tears fall out of the eye.

generic term

occasional use of passive voice

In order to see an object, we need to look at it. *Muscles* of both eyes move in the direction of the object, making sure that both eyes move together. Covering a sixth of the eye's surface is the *cornea*. The cornea is a domed window which lets light from the object into the eye. It also bends the light coming in, helping to focus the light through the pupil. The *pupil* is a hole through which light enters the middle and back of the eye.

separate paragraphs for different parts of the explanation

Surrounding the pupil is the thin, coloured *iris*. *Ciliary muscles* at the side of the eye contract or expand the iris depending on how much light is available. When the light is low, then the iris will contract, making the pupil larger and so allowing more light to enter the eye. If there is a lot of light the iris will expand, making the pupil smaller so that too much light does not enter the eye and damage it.

complex sentence

causal connective

Just behind the pupil is the *lens*. The lens helps to focus light into a sharp image on the *retina* at the back of the eyeball. Sometimes the lens becomes stiff and cannot bend or curve sufficiently to create this sharp image. Because of this, some people wear glasses which have artificial lenses that correct the vision.

technical language (in italics)

In the middle of the eyeball is a thick, transparent, jelly-like substance called the *vitreous humour*. This fluid helps to keep the eyeball in its correct shape and allows the light coming into the eye to reach the back of the eyeball to the retina.

third person

The retina is an inner layer of the eyeball. It is very sensitive to light. Cells in the retina, called *rods* and *cones*, convert light into nerve impulses. The retinal nerves come together to form the *optic nerve* which goes to the visual centre of the brain. The brain then interprets the messages received and we can then recognise and describe the object we are looking at.

present tense

Light, then, is essential to sight as the eye is designed to receive, bend and transfer light into images for the brain to interpret.

closing statement

HOW OUR EYES WORK

Sight is the most highly developed sense in humans. Eyes are receptors to light reflected from objects and the brain interprets these reflections into objects that we recognise. The eye itself does not produce any light and so without light we would not be able to see. Light sources can be primary, that is, they give out light directly, for example, the sun or a torch or secondary, that is, they reflect light from a primary source, for example, mirrors.

The eye is like a small round ball that sits in the **eye socket**. It is protected by the *conjunctiva, eyelashes, eyelids* and *tear ducts*. The conjunctiva is a thin protective membrane that covers the front of the eyeball and lines the eyelids. Eyelashes stop particles of dust entering the eye. The eyelids are closed frequently by blinking. This action maintains a moist film over the eye that enables it to move freely and also protects the main parts from dust. Tear ducts produce a salty liquid that acts as a cleansing agent for the eye. When humans cry, an excess of this liquid is produced so tears fall out of the eye.

In order to see an object, we need to look at it. Muscles of both eyes move in the direction of the object, making sure that both eyes move together. Covering a sixth of the eye's surface is the *cornea*. The cornea is a domed window which lets light from the object into the eye. It also bends the light coming in, helping to focus the light through the pupil. The *pupil* is a hole through which light enters the middle and back of the eye.

Surrounding the pupil is the thin, coloured *iris*. *Ciliary muscles* at the side of the eye contract or expand the iris depending on how much light is available. When the light is low, then the iris will contract, making the pupil larger and so allowing more light to enter the eye. If there is a lot of light the iris will expand, making the pupil smaller so that too much light does not enter the eye and damage it.

Just behind the pupil is the *lens*. The lens helps to focus light into a sharp image on the *retina* at the back of the eyeball. Sometimes the lens becomes stiff and cannot bend or curve sufficiently to create this sharp image. Because of this, some people wear glasses which have artificial lenses that correct the vision.

In the middle of the eyeball is a thick, transparent, jelly-like substance called the *vitreous humour*. This fluid helps to keep the eyeball in its correct shape and allows the light coming into the eye to reach the back of the eyeball to the retina.

The retina is an inner layer of the eyeball. It is very sensitive to light. Cells in the retina, called *rods* and *cones*, convert light into nerve impulses. The retinal nerves come together to form the *optic nerve* which goes to the visual centre of the brain. The brain then interprets the messages received and we can then recognise and describe the object we are looking at.

Light, then, is essential to sight as the eye is designed to receive, bend and transfer light into images for the brain to interpret.

Parts of the eye

Use the words in the box to label the diagram below.

optic nerve	iris	eyelash	vitreous humour
retina	cornea	lens	eyelid	conjunctiva
pupil	eye muscle	ciliary muscle	

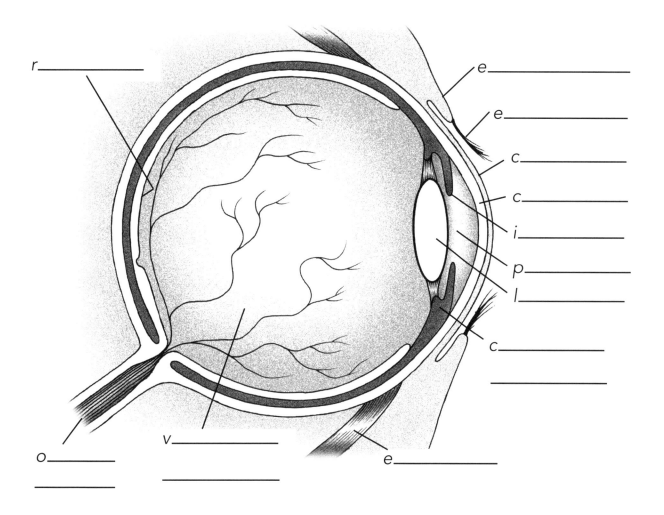

The science bit

Light travels in a straight line from a source.

A mirror is backed by material that is opaque. This stops the light travelling through the transparent glass of the mirror, making the mirror reflective.

The light hits the mirror and bounces back off.

The light bouncing off the mirror still travels in a straight line, but can reflect off the mirror at different angles, depending on how the mirror is tilted.

The reflection travels to our eyes and we see it.

The image we see is back to front.

Chapter 5

Persuasion writing

What is a persuasion text?

A persuasion text argues the case for a belief or issue from a particular point of view. The point of view is supported by evidence and reasoning.

Examples of persuasive texts include: advertisements, travel brochures, letters to express a point of view.

Structural features

■ Usually begins with an opening statement to indicate the point of view to be expressed

■ Main body of text lists the arguments for the point of view supported by evidence and reasoning

■ Ends with a conclusion that reiterates the opening statement and presents a summary of the arguments presented.

Linguistic features

■ Present tense

■ General terms usually used (such as 'people should' rather than 'Mr Jones should')

■ Use of connectives to show logic (therefore, however, because of, due to, despite, this shows, in spite of, as a result of)

■ Often uses rhetorical questions addressed directly to the reader (Can you believe?)

■ Alliterative sentences (in advertisements especially)

■ Emotive and persuasive language

■ Use of pictures/illustrations to gain an emotional response from the reader

Teaching persuasion writing

It is incredibly easy for children to express their opinions but giving reasons for these opinions is not so simple! Children need lots of oral practice in determining the reasons behind their opinions before they can begin to write them.

When writing persuasively children need to know their subject well and be able to provide supporting evidence (facts or believable fiction) as well as predicting any possible counter arguments. It is vital that they have lots of opportunities to read examples of persuasion writing in order to be able to identify the features and evaluate the success of different persuasive devices before actually trying them out themselves.

The purpose of the text is of the utmost importance. What does the writer want the reader to do in response? Having a clear idea of the proposed outcome will ensure the children experience more successful planning and completion of the writing.

Persuasion writing – progression

Persuasive texts are introduced in Year 3 through letter writing (Term 3: T16).

In Year 4 children read, compare and evaluate examples of arguments; look at how arguments are presented and how statistics and graphs can be used to support arguments and investigate how style and vocabulary are used to convince the reader (Term 3: T16, T17, T18). They assemble and sequence points in order to plan the presentation of a point of view, using writing frames to back up points of view with illustrations and examples and to present the point of view in the form of a letter, script or report (Term 3: T21, T22, T23). They evaluate adverts for their impact, appeal and honesty and design their own (Term 3: T19, T25).

In Year 5 children read and evaluate letters intended to persuade. They collect and investigate persuasive devices. They write group letters for real issues, write commentaries on an issue and construct and present an argument to the class (Term 3: T12, T14, T15, T17, T18, T19).

In **Year 6** the focus moves on to recognising how effective arguments are constructed and actually constructing one, themselves (Term 2: T15, T16, T18).

Unit 1

Lesson focus

History Unit 19 – What were the effects of Tudor exploration?

Overall aim

To write a persuasive letter of complaint to Queen Elizabeth I from the Native American perspective of the Roanoke settlement.

History emphasis

In this unit the children will learn that settlement in other countries is not always as straightforward as it may seem. The children will be encouraged to relate what they have learned to current issues – learning about the Roanoke settlement could raise questions about subsequent times, such as the building of the British Empire and provide them with some insights into the debates about refugees today.

Literacy links

Year 6, Term 2: T15, T18

About this unit

This unit could be undertaken with a literacy link by using Shakespeare's *The Tempest* as this play has colonisation of other people's islands as part of its plot. The programme of study for Key Stage 2 History requires children to understand that the past is represented and interpreted in different ways and to be able to give reasons for this. By going beyond the factual evidence and imagining the points of view of the settlers and the Native Americans, the children will be able to gather that history is often not simply a knowledge based subject, but one which calls for the higher order thinking skills of synthesis and evaluation. In literacy, they should have done some work on persuasive writing and understand that its purpose is to convince the reader of a point of view. The children will need to have studied the Roanoke settlement in their history lessons before they begin the lessons in this unit.

Switching on

Learning objectives

■ To improvise the events of the Roanoke settlement.

■ To begin to formulate opinions about the Roanoke settlement.

Resources

■ Sheet A (pages 88 and 89)

What to do

These activities could spread over several lessons.

Try and begin the lesson in a dramatic way by marching into class and announcing that you have just heard some news. Tell the children that the headteacher has told you that lots of children from another country are going to come to England and join them in their school. If they like the school, there is a chance that their families will join them and settle in the area. Tell the children that each class will have a large group of these children. They will have to share their space, equipment, playground and

lessons. Tell them that you have heard that these children have been taught in a different way and are exceptionally good at maths and literacy, but have not had many lessons in sport and have never seen English television. Say that you are a bit stunned, but that the headteacher wants to know their immediate reactions and that they are to write down how they feel and if they have any objections. Explain that they will be writing anonymously so no one will know who wrote what – this way they can say what they really think about the situation.

Try to appear a bit harassed and unsure yourself. In response to any of the children's questions, simply say that you have told them all you know. Allow the children some time to discuss their responses and then tell them all to start writing how they feel and what they think.

When the children have finished, ask them to fold their pieces of paper up to keep what they have written secret. Collect it in and then tell them that they are now going

to begin their history lesson about the Roanoke settlement while you read their responses in order to report back to the headteacher.

Divide the class into six groups and give each child a copy of Sheet A. Explain that you want them to read both sheets and to discuss as a group how the English and the Native Americans might have felt about each other.

While they do this read their written responses and note any strong negative or positive reactions.

After a while, stop the class. Tell them that you have told them a whopping big fib! Tell them that no children are coming to the school and that you did this to see what sort of responses you would get from them. If there were any strong responses, discuss these with the children and relate them to how the Native Americans might have felt when the English people arrived in Roanoke. Discuss how the English settlers might have felt about landing in a strange place, far from home and meeting people who were very different from themselves.

Discuss Sheet A in general, making sure the children have understood the text. Now explain that you want them to work in their groups and decide how to improvise parts of the story of the Roanoke settlement. Allocate one section of Sheet A to each group. Each section has at least four people in the cast and, depending on the size of your class, there are possibilities for the children to be members of the tribes, sailors or colonists. Each group is to cast themselves and dramatise the events of their section. Tell them that when they have made up their drama, the whole story will be performed in sequence.

Before they begin, agree some rules for the group task. Write them on the board. They could include:

One person speaks at a time;

Everyone else listens;

Everyone takes turns to speak;

Everyone in the group votes if there is a disagreement;

Everyone is given a task to do;

Everyone does their task to the best of their ability;

If you have to wait while someone else is doing something, be still and quiet;

Accept things when they don't go your way;

If you disagree with something, put your hand up and wait to be listened to. When the group are listening to you, speak quietly;

Make sure that you are doing everything you can to make your group produce the best work.

To begin with, the children can work in the classroom, casting and working out what sort of things each member of the cast can do to dramatise the events in their section. When they are ready, they could be taken to the school hall to 'act out' their improvisations and make adjustments.

While the children are working on their improvisations, visit every group and ensure that all the children are working cooperatively.

Stop the class every ten minutes or so to allow a different group to 'show' how far their improvisation has come along. The other children in the class can comment and provide suggestions for improvement.

It would give the children a stronger sense of motivation if they thought their finished improvisations were going to be performed for someone, so try to arrange for them to show the story during an assembly or for another class or arrange for the story to be filmed on video.

Plenary

After the children have performed the whole story, evaluate their performances with them. Then ask the children to work in their performance groups to come up with one sentence that describes the Native Americans and one sentence that describes the English.

Revving up

Learning objectives

■ To investigate the structural and linguistic features of a persuasive text.

Resources

■ Sheets B and C (pages 90 and 91)
■ Scissors, glue, large sheets of paper

What to do

Before this lesson: enlarge a copy of Sheet B. Age the letter. (Pat it with cold tea bags and allow it to dry. Then burn the edges with a match, knocking off any totally charred paper.) Roll the letter up and put a ribbon around it.

Tell the children you have a special letter to read to them. Unroll the prepared Sheet B and stick it to the white board. Read the letter to the children. Ask them who they think the letter is from (referring back to 'Switching on' if necessary). Remind them that what became of the Roanoke settlers is still a mystery. Tell them that some people think they were all killed by the Native Americans, but that there is a strong possibility that they were taken to Croatoan and became part of the Native American tribe. Discuss for a while what this must have been like.

Ask the children for their opinions about the letter by asking questions such as *'Does Virginia sound happy?,' 'What clues are there that the English are beginning to join in with the Native Americans?', 'What clues are there that the English are trying to stay English?'*

Ask the children that if they were Queen Elizabeth 1 and had received the letter and there was no war with Spain,

would it persuade them to send help? Discuss the term 'persuasive' and ask them if they can find anything in the letter that they think is persuasive.

Tell them that they are going to investigate the letter further to identify what bits of it make it persuasive. Divide the children into pairs and provide them with their own copy of Sheet B plus a copy of Sheet C. Ask different children to read out each speech bubble on Sheet C. Discuss the terms used, for example 'generic' and 'rhetorical', to make sure they understand the meaning of each speech bubble.

Ask the children to work in pairs to find an example of each speech bubble in the letter. Tell them that after they have identified the examples, they are to stick the letter onto a larger piece of coloured paper, cut out the speech bubbles and stick them around the outside of the letter so that the pointers on the speech bubbles are pointing to the examples of that feature in the text.

While the children are doing this, sit with a group of less able children and challenge them to find as many examples as they can. Then challenge them to find alternative ways of writing each example.

Plenary

Ask the children which speech bubbles provide structural features and which provide linguistic features. Tell them that during a later lesson they are going to write a persuasive letter to Queen Elizabeth 1, only this time it will be from the perspective of the Native Americans and it will be a letter of complaint. Ask the children what complaints the Native Americans have – refer back to 'Switching on' and their improvisations if necessary. Ask them to do some research at school or home – to research the story further and to find out as much as possible about the lives and customs of the Native Americans.

Taking off

Learning objectives

■ To experiment with persuasive language.

■ To identify key points that may account for the Native American perspective at the Roanoke settlement.

Resources

■ A collection of advertisements

■ Materials for making posters – paper and felt tips

What to do

Tell the children that today they are going to prepare a poster for a demonstration march on behalf of the Native Americans of Roanoke!

Refer back to any information the children may have gathered through research and the 'Switching on' lesson and ask them to give you ideas why the Native Americans may feel very upset about their treatment at the hands of the English. Write their ideas on the board.

Show the children the advertisements and ask them to tell you what they notice about them. What makes the advertisements effective? (Slogans, bright colours, repetition, alliteration and humour.) What persuasive devices do they use?

Briefly discuss television advertisements. Ask them how long they think they last (many are approximately 30 seconds long). Explain that advertisements have to catch people's attention very quickly and stick in their minds.

Tell them their job is to think up a poster for the march that will do almost the same job as an advertisement – they have to make a poster that will catch the attention of people who are watching the protest march.

Refer back to their ideas on the board. Explain that they need to decide on which point they wish to make their poster about (or if they wish they can sum them all up in one sentence). Tell them that once they have decided on this, they have to make up a slogan that will convey the message. Point out how this has been done on the advertisements you have (for example, 'Everyone needs a Tetley moment'). Remind them of the linguistic features of persuasive texts and ask them to try and incorporate some of these in their posters (for example, present tense, emotional language, rhetorical questions).

Ask the children to plan their posters. They could work in pairs. They could use reference books on Native Americans to find designs to use in their poster (such as those on their totem poles or other artefacts). Suggest that these could be used as borders, for example. Remind them that these are protest posters against the Native American treatment by the English of Roanoke.

While they are planning their posters, go round the class, making suggestions and helping as necessary. Stop the class from time to time to point out any good ideas that have been generated. Remind the children to use the linguistic features you have discussed earlier.

Before the children make their final copies of the posters, ask them to work with another pair to share ideas about how their poster design could be improved. Ask them to especially check that their poster is persuasive.

Plenary

When the posters are ready, ask the children to come up with a poster chant (for example, 'Native Americans in, English out,' or 'Keep America free of Invaders'). They could march around the playground with their posters, saying their chants. When you are back in the classroom, ask the children to vote for the posters that should go up on display. Before they vote, remind the children that what you are looking for are posters that are the most persuasive about the Native Americans perspective of the Roanoke settlement.

Flying solo

Learning objectives

■ To write a persuasive letter.

Resources

■ Sheet B (page 90)
■ Children's work from 'Revving up'

What to do

Remind the children about the letter they read in 'Revving up'. Tell them that they are going to write their own letter to Queen Elizabeth I pretending they are Native Americans at the time or just after the Roanoke settlement events. Explain that the letter needs to try and persuade the Queen that her representatives have behaved badly and should be punished.

Remind them about the features of a persuasive text explored in 'Revving up' and tell them that they can refer to their sheets they made in order to help them write their letters. You could also put on display a copy of Sheet B.

Have a quick discussion about the points that the Native Americans might feel angry about.

Tell the children that you are now going to model writing the opening of a letter from an Native American. What follows is for your eyes only to use or adapt as you wish. What you say is written in italics, what you write is written in bold.

What I have to think about is the Native American perspective. How would they have viewed the events? What was their life like and how would they imagine Queen Elizabeth I and England? Let me see, they wouldn't have gone to an English school and they would probably think Elizabeth was a bit like their chiefs. I also need to think about the layout, structural features and the persuasiveness

of my letter. I wouldn't really know the date, so I'll make up a sort of time and an address.

Roanoke Island

Land of Brothers

Day of Corn ripening

How would they address the Queen? They may have some help from an English settler.

Dear Important Queen

I need to start with an opening that states the overall case.

My brothers and sisters greet you from our land. It is a land where our ancestors' spirits have been since the creation of our people. We honour this land by growing food for ourselves and respecting the spirits that provide this food. We were happy to share this land with your brothers and sisters that came across the oceans of the world to be here.

Now, I've made the case that this land belonged to the Native Americans and that they knew how to use the land properly. I've also said that the Native Americans were glad to share it with others. Now I have to say something about what went wrong.

Though we greeted our visitors with warm hearts, they took from us without repayment. They killed our kinsfolk, burned our villages and treated us without honour. Only a coward would not defend themselves against such discourtesy.

If I were to carry on I would now go on to spell out two or three things that were done by the English and why the response from the Native Americans was in reaction to this. I would try and persuade Queen Elizabeth that I was a reasonable and honourable person in an impossible situation.

But first, let me look at what I have written. I have opened the letter with a statement that indicates my point of view. I have begun to list my arguments and provided evidence and reasoning. I have used generic terms like 'visitors' and I have used emotive and persuasive language such as 'warm hearts' and 'only a coward would…'

Ask the children to look at what you have written and suggest improvements if they can.

Then ask them to work individually on their persuasive letters of complaint. Sit with a less able group and do some shared writing of a composite letter, making sure that they follow each step of the structural features and incorporate the linguistic features.

The completed letters can be 'aged' if you wish. They could be rolled up, tied with a ribbon put into bottles ('messages in a bottle' from 16th Century America).

Plenary

Ask an adult (preferably one with a commanding presence) to come into class and pretend to be Queen Elizabeth 1. Choose some children to present their letters to her. She is to read the letters out and make comments upon them (for example, 'what terrible spelling, these Native Americans have not been taught in one of my schools' or 'how dare they address me in this fashion'). Then she is to point out any really persuasive comments, expressions and so on and dramatise being moved by the letters and persuaded by them that her representatives abroad have behaved very badly and should have their heads cut off.

1. CAST: Sir Walter Raleigh, Queen Elizabeth I, Simon Fernando, Spanish narrator

EVENTS: The Spanish have become wealthy. They have explored America and taken gold and other goods from the Native Americans. The English often attack Spanish ships to steal the gold and goods. The English want to build a colony in America so that they can get the gold and the goods for themselves and also to make America a part of England. Queen Elizabeth and Sir Walter Raleigh decide to send Simon Fernando to America to find a good place for an English colony. Simon Fernando has been to America before.

2. CAST: Native American King Wingina and his tribe, Simon Fernando, English sailors

EVENTS: Simon Fernando and his sailors find a place called Roanoke in America and they think it is a good place for English colonists to settle. They meet King Wingina and his tribe. The English and the Native Americans do not speak each other's language and there are confusions. For example, the English ask the Native Americans what the place is called. The Native Americans say 'Wingandacon' which means 'I like your clothes.' The English and the Native Americans exchange gifts and visits. There are lots of parties, both on land and on ship. Simon Fernando and his sailors decide that they will go back to England and tell everyone that they have found a good place where the natives are friendly and helpful.

3. CAST: Sir Richard Grenville, Ralph Lane, English explorers, Native Americans

EVENTS: Sir Richard Grenville, Ralph Lane and English explorers arrive in Roanoke. They build a strong fort and houses. The explorers find the Native Americans highly civilised, good farmers and able to survive off the land. However, Sir Richard and Ralph Lane think the Native Americans are savages and they prefer to steal from them rather than learn from them. They steal food and burn their villages. Ralph Lane kidnaps an Native American leader and keeps his son in prison for months. Sir Richard returns to England.

4. CAST: Sir Francis Drake, Native Americans, Ralph Lane, soldiers

EVENTS: The Native Americans are angry at the way they have been treated and refuse to help the English in any way. The English become hungry. Sir Francis Drake arrives in Roanoke and decides to take the English back home, but to leave some soldiers to watch over the Roanoke settlement. The Native Americans see the ship sail away, leaving just a few soldiers behind!

5. CAST: John White, Simon Fernando, Native Americans, English colonists who include John White's daughter

EVENTS: Simon Fernando returns to Roanoke with lots of men, women and children. John White is to be in charge. They find that the soldiers that were left behind have all disappeared – apart from a few bones! Fernando knows it is dangerous but he leaves the English colonists in Roanoke so that he can go off and steal from a few more Spanish ships. The colonists fight with the natives, steal their food and attack their villages. A colonist gets killed by the Native Americans. John White's daughter has a baby girl called 'Virginia'. She is the first English person to be born on American soil. The colonists run out of food and are very frightened of the Native Americans. They send John White back to England for help.

6. CAST: John White, pirate, Queen Elizabeth i, Sir Walter Raleigh

EVENTS:John White pleads with Queen Elizabeth and Sir Walter Raleigh to send supplies and help to the colonists in Roanoke, but the English are now at war with Spain. Queen Elizabeth and Sir Walter say that all their ships are needed to defeat the Spanish Armada. After three years, John White finds a pirate to take him back to Roanoke. There is no one there. There is a carving on a tree that says 'CROATOAN'. Croatoan is a place not too far from Roanoke. Does this mean that the colonists have moved there? Or have they all been killed by the Native americans? There is a terrible hurricane and the pirate refuses to go to Croatoan and forces John White to return to England. The colonists have never been found.

May, 1599

Croatoan,
Hatteras Island,
America.

Most Worshipful and Gracious Majesty,

It is with much humility and pardon that I write to your most revered self. It is only the anguish and despair that we, your most faithful subjects, feel, that allows me to dare approach you. Twelve years ago I came into being on Roanoke Island, your first humble subject born on American soil. Soon after my birth, my grandfather, John White returned to beloved England to beseech you to help our beleaguered colony. Since then, we have been taken and forced to live among the savages, here at Croatoan. In all that time, though we stare seaward every hour, we have not seen the brave men you most assuredly must have sent to rescue us. I am determined to put this letter in a bottle and trust to the Lord that it sails across the oceans and lands in your most compassionate hands. As a result I most desperately pray that you will remember us and manage our return to live in England under your protection.

Since I have never seen England I can only listen to the tales of my people and compare their stories with the existence I know. Who could doubt the wonders of your realm? Music, theatre, costumes, jewels, food to be bought from shops, carriages - all these things are not known to me and people weep when they recall them. Therefore, should their memories be their only source of comfort, their only sense of being at home, of belonging? After all, your colonists are born and bred to live in the way you desired of them. They struggle to remain faithful to your example.

However, it is mighty hard not to behave like our captors when day by day we are fed, clothed and entertained by them. Only a fool would think wrong of someone who occasionally painted their faces with dye to cheer themselves up. How could a lonely man resist the friendship of a female savage? Yet we berate ourselves for every turn away from the behaviour we know is acceptable to you. It is desperately important that we are removed from here before we are not distinguishable from these natives. Is it to be imagined that, as a result of living here, your most worthy subjects turn into savages? In years to come, will people say that Queen Elizabeth, the most illustrious monarch God has ever given to the world, had savages among her peoples?

I therefore beseech you to send moral and spiritual salvation to us by way of ships and doughty men who will fight off the natives that keep us and who will return us to our rightful place in England. My faith in God and in you will keep me looking towards the horizon until such time as we are rescued.

I remain your faithful and humble servant,

VIRGINIA DARE

Sheet C

An opening statement that tells the reader what the argument (case) is about.

Argument for the case with reasons.

Argument against the case with a counter argument (for example, 'Some people may say… however…')

Mostly written in the present tense.

Logical connective (for example, therefore, however, consequently, after all, since, moreover, on the other hand, finally, as a result of, yet).

An ending that says again what the main point of view is.

Generic term (for example, 'people' rather than 'my mother').

Rhetorical question.

Emotional language (for example, 'desperate').

Persuasive language (for example, 'only a fool would think that...' or 'anyone with any sense would agree that...').

Unit 2

Lesson focus

Citizenship Unit 10 – Local democracy for young citizens

Overall aim

To write a manifesto persuading other children to vote for them as members of a school council.

Citizenship emphasis

In this unit the children explore issues of democracy where they begin to understand their rights and responsibilities as part of a community. By practising their democratic rights the children will begin to appreciate how these rights belong to all members of the community, not just those people who have the same beliefs and aspirations as themselves. Learning how to persuade logically and imaginatively by writing a manifesto provides the children with a valuable 'real' experience in the processes of a democracy and can have a lasting impact on their lives in the community.

Literacy links

Year 6, Term 2: T15, T18

About this unit

The children should be familiar with the features of persuasive writing (see the beginning of this chapter) and have had experience of a range of persuasive texts.

These sessions would be best taught during PSHE and Citizenship and should follow an initial discussion about the roles and responsibilities of each member of a community. The children will be using analytical and reflective thinking skills to make judgements about leadership. They will also be making decisions about their own leadership qualities.

Switching on

Learning objectives

■ To explore qualities of leadership.

■ To answer questions and make notes.

■ To generate ideas for a personal manifesto.

Resources

■ Sheet A (page 97)

■ Information sources about the lives of famous leaders

What to do

This lesson could spread over several sessions.

Tell the children that they are going to find out about the lives of some famous leaders in order to identify how these people became leaders and what qualities they had that made people want to follow them. Briefly discuss the children's perception of famous leaders. How many can they name? What qualities do they think a good leader needs? Why?

Organise the class into five groups. Give each group a leader to research (for example, Thatcher, Gandhi, Hitler, Mother Teresa, Nelson Mandela, Jesus Christ) and provide them with information sources to use. Find out what they already know about these people first. Write up their ideas on a flip chart so that they can be referred to later.

Ask each group to answer the following questions through their research.

1. What were the circumstances that led to this person becoming a leader?

2. What were the qualities this person had that made people follow him or her?

3. Was their leadership beneficial to society and if so, in what way?

The groups could be organised to work in different ways. For example, all the children in the group could read the information and make notes, then come together to produce a final product. Or the children could work in

pairs within the groups - one reading, one making notes and then share what they found out with others in their group.

When the children have finished this work, create a 'jigsaw' organisation of the class. One way of doing this is to give each group a number (group 1, group 2). All the children in each group will become an expert on the leader they have been researching. So, for example, group 1 may have been researching Margaret Thatcher. Ask each member of the group to split up and go to a different group and tell them what they have found out in answer to the three questions. The children in the other groups should be encouraged to ask them questions and discuss with them, for example, the qualities of leadership found in Margaret Thatcher. After ten minutes, ask group 1 to return to their seats, then ask group 2 to split up and go to the other groups and repeat the task, until all groups have had a turn.

An alternative method is to give each child in each group a letter, for example, child A, child B, and so on. Ask all the 'child A' children to gather together and share their information, all the 'child B' children to gather together and share their information and so on.

When all the groups have finished sharing their information, gather the class together and ask the children to go through the original questions and discuss them. Ask them if there are qualities of leadership that appear common to all the people they have been researching. Together, create a 'composite' generic leader that incorporates all the best qualities of leadership. You could draw an outline of a head on the board and fill it with the words generated and display it in the classroom.

Tell the children that they are now going to put their knowledge about leadership qualities to use. Explain that you want them to imagine they have been nominated for a position on the School Council. Discuss the purpose of a School Council and what a manifesto is. (If you really do have a School Council, carry out this unit of work at the time of council elections.) Explain that the purpose of the manifesto is to persuade other children to vote for them.

Refer back to the first question they explored for the famous leaders. Ask them if they think there are circumstances in the school that need addressing. What things do they think they could improve/change that would make people want to vote for them? Allow them some time to think about this and then explain that you have a list of ideas that might help them decide.

Hand out copies of Sheet A. Explain that they are going to go through the ideas to see if any of them relate to their school and to add any others that they think need addressing.

Read through the list together. Ask the children to consider those ideas they think would be popular and therefore gain 'votes' if they were incorporated into their own manifestoes.

Tell them that you want them to make their own list now – just three or four points at the most – those they feel most strongly about. Explain that this is because a manifesto is more persuasive if it focuses on a limited number of points and that all successful leaders have the quality of believing passionately about their own points of view. The ideas can be taken from the sheet or they can generate their own.

While the children are working on this, sit with a group of lower ability children and share reading Sheet A again. Help them choose two or three ideas for their own manifestoes.

Plenary

Ask a confident child to tell the class what points or issues they have chosen to incorporate into their manifesto. Ask the child to defend their choice and to say why these were chosen and not others. Point out any aspects of the following from this child; logical reasoning, clear articulation, choosing a good vote winner, clear arguments against alternative choices, strong belief in the choices.

Revving up

Learning objectives

■ To investigate the key features of a persuasive text.

Resources

■ Sheets B and C (pages 98 and 99)

What to do

Tell the children that they are going to read an example of a child's election speech for the School Council in order to help them write their own one later.

Share an enlarged version of Sheet C. Ask them to tell you what they think the purpose of this text is (to persuade people to vote for the person who wrote it). Do they consider the author to have been successful in trying to persuade them? Why/why not?

Next, consider the structural features of the text. Ask the children to comment on the layout, asking questions such as: 'How many paragraphs does it have?', 'What does each paragraph do?', 'How does it start?', 'How does it end?', 'How effective is this layout?' and 'What changes would they make if any?'

Make a list of the structural features on the board or flip chart. Include: introduction/opening statement to tell the reader the point of view that is going to be presented, paragraphs that list the arguments for the point of view, conclusion/closing statement that sums up the point of view.

Now ask them to look carefully at the words and phrases that are used. Ask the children to tell you which words and phrases in the text they think are persuasive and to explain why.

Go through the other linguistic features of the text, using Sheet B as your guide. Explain any unfamiliar terms such as 'rhetorical', making sure the children understand the meaning of the terms. Make a list of these features: present tense, rhetorical questions, emotive and persuasive language, logical connectives.

Hand out copies of Sheet C to the children. Ask them to work in pairs to annotate the text according to the list of features on the board. They could use highlighters or underline/circle words and phrases. How many logical connectives can they find? How many examples of emotive/persuasive words?

Walk around the classroom while the children are doing this, ensuring that they have understood what they are supposed to do. Make suggestions and compliment the children where you find good work. Stop the class from time to time to see how everyone is getting on and to respond to any general difficulties.

Plenary

Share what the children have found out. You could display an enlarged version of Sheet B as a guide. Did they find phrases that make the reader feel foolish if they do not agree with the writer? ('People with any sense realise...') Why do they think the writer of a persuasive text might do this? Ask them to come up with some other ideas for how they could make the reader feel foolish for not agreeing with them.

Taking off

Learning objectives

- To draft a manifesto.
- To evaluate themselves as leaders.

Resources

- Children's lists of manifesto ideas from 'Switching on'
- Checklist of features from 'Revving up'

What to do

Refer back to 'Switching on' and ask the children to reiterate the leadership qualities they identified. Ask them to write down three qualities they think they have that would make them good leaders. Explain that these qualities may not be obvious ones for good leadership, but that qualities such as helpfulness, kindness, being funny and so on can be included.

Sit the children in a circle and ask each child to choose another child to say something nice about – in terms of benefit to the school, such as being a good friend or being helpful/kind to others. Once a child has been picked by someone, they cannot be chosen again. Go round the circle again and ask the children what qualities they identified in themselves and if others agree.

Tell them that they are now going to plan their manifesto. Remind them of the example one they read in the previous lesson and tell them that the manifesto must include the qualities that would make them a good leader as well as the ideas for the school that would get them votes. Tell them that they could organise their planning under three headings: 'My leadership qualities', 'My ideas for the school' and 'Persuasive words and phrases I will use'.

When they have finished this, ask some children to read out their notes and discuss them by either pointing out what may not work or stressing what is a good idea and extending by adding any ideas that come to mind or that other children can suggest.

Plenary

Ask the children to sit with a partner and share their plans. Do they think their partner can add/amend anything? Can they suggest better emotive and persuasive words/phrases?

Tell the children that they are going to 'perform' their manifesto to others. Ask them to think about how they will make their talk sound convincing to others. Suggest that they practise what they might say at home.

Flying solo

Learning objectives

- To write a manifesto.
- To give a prepared speech.

Resources

- Children's plans from 'Taking off'

What to do

Tell the children that they are going to use their plans to write their manifestoes. Explain that you are going to model how they can do this.

What follows is for your eyes only to use or adapt as you wish. What you say is written in italics and what you write is written in bold.

I want to persuade other teachers to vote for me as King/Queen teacher. I shall start by using an opening statement that tells them what I am writing about and why I should be chosen.

Although I have only been in this school for ... years, I believe I should be voted as King/Queen teacher. Not only do I have all the qualities of a King/Queen, but my rule will benefit everyone in the school.

Now, I have stated what this text is going to be about and I have given my overall reasons why I should be chosen. I am now going to have to say what qualities I have that make me the best person for King/Queen teacher.

A King/Queen teacher needs to be able to order other people around successfully. I have proved that I am the bossiest person in the school and I am famous for enjoying being in charge. Not only this, but I am the only person in the school who has developed the knack of looking down my nose at others. It is obvious to anyone with any brains that looking down one's nose is a vital factor in being King/Queen of anything.

Ask the children what factors, structural or linguistic they can find in your writing. Ask them what they think you should write about next and what other linguistic features you could use. Continue writing for a few more paragraphs.

Send the children off to write their own manifestoes. Remind them to remember to persuade others to vote for them and to include the list of things they want to improve in the school and say how they will do this.

Work with a group of children who need more support – perhaps drafting a group manifesto.

After about 20 minutes, stop the class and share some of the introductory paragraphs. Remind them about the need to include a summing up paragraph at the end. Ask them to share their manifestoes with a partner. Display the features checklist and ask the partners to tick each feature found. Do they need to add/amend their texts in the light of this?

You could arrange for the children to try out their manifestoes on the rest of the school before they complete their final drafts. This could be done by letting the other classes know that several children from your class will be reading out their manifestoes in the playground over the coming week. Prepare your class for this by discussing how this should be done. Tell them that

reading aloud needs certain techniques and that they should be aware of the following:

Read slowly;

Project your voice to the back of the crowd;

Read slightly ahead of what you are saying;

Look up at the crowd frequently as you read;

Emphasise key words and phrases;

Use arm movements sparingly, but dramatically;

Make sure you can be heard, but try not to shout.

Let the children take pens out with them so that they can make further alterations if they discover they need to make changes after reading their manifestoes aloud.

Plenary

Share the children's ideas about the process of preparing a manifesto and finally presenting it. How passionate are they about their ideas – has it made them want to make changes in the school? Do they think a School Council is a good idea in order to make these changes? How important is it to be given the opportunity to express your views and to hear the views of others?

Sheet A

Manifesto ideas

I propose the following ideas

Playtime

To introduce more play equipment, to have designated areas for different activities and to have a buddy system.

Year 6

To have more responsibilities such as showing visitors around and leading assemblies. (Concessions for these responsibilities to include time in the classroom at playtime.) To set up an area designated for Year 6. To have a day off school uniform once a term.

Environment

To create areas for wildlife such as a school pond or meadow. To improve display areas and display boards. To have litter patrols.

Rules

To have a say in developing the school rules and to decide on rewards and sanctions.

Bullying

To have a say in what is considered to be bullying and how the school should deal with it.

Learning

To have opportunities to learn in ways that suit different people.

Equipment

To raise funds to get rid of old/boring books and buy new ones, replacing old paintbrushes and so on.

Charity

To organise charity tables in the playground once a week.

Snack Shop

To introduce a snack shop once a week, run by children.

opening statement

Changes: not for the better – but for the best!
I have been in this school for three years now. During that time I have come to know what changes should be made to improve the many tedious hours we spend here. Anyone who knows me will agree that I am the best person to represent Class 6 on the School Council. It is time for you to choose the one person who can make the changes you want happen – not just changes for the better, but changes to make this school the best!

present tense

arguments for the case

Some of you may ask what qualities I have that make me the obvious choice for school councillor. First of all, I would make it my policy to listen to any suggestions you put forward. My role would be to represent your feelings and ideas. Surely we do not want people who refuse to listen to other people's ideas? We all know those ignorant people who never take the time to find out how other people think. Would they give you the chance to influence what goes on in the school? On the contrary, with me, if you have something to say, let me say it for you on the council.

arguments against the case

persuasive language

Most of you will be aware that I am not afraid about speaking up. This may also be true of others who want your vote. The difference is, that I am able to speak up without causing offence to adults or other children. As a result, I am adept at getting others to agree to a point of view. People with any sense realise that this essential quality of mine is the most likely to succeed in getting changes made. Imagine how some of the people who are asking for your vote would behave. Some would never speak up, some would bore everyone by not being able to put their views across and some would simply be so rude, their views would not be listened to.

emotive language

logical connective

Moreover, although your ideas and suggestions will be an important element of my role on the council, what is also needed is a strong leader that can make fantastic changes happen. The person you elect must have brilliant ideas of their own and be strong enough to carry them through. My manifesto demonstrates the sort of new ideas that I will be putting forward to make this school the best. It is true that some of you will have your own ideas, but you will find that mine are exciting and these are just the beginnings!

These are my ideas... (Here the author lists the ideas for the school.)

Choosing the right person to represent you on the School Council is your chance to influence changes that will improve your experiences at school. Do you want to waste this chance? You should choose someone who will listen to you, speak well and who has great ideas of their own. I am the only person who fits this description. Vote for me and you will be voting for changes that don't just make things better – but make changes for the best!

persuasive language

rhetorical question

concluding statement

Sheet C

Changes: not for the better – but for the best!

I have been in this school for three years now. During that time I have come to know what changes should be made to improve the many tedious hours we spend here. Anyone who knows me will agree that I am the best person to represent Class 6 on the School Council. It is time for you to choose the one person who can make the changes you want happen – not just changes for the better, but changes to make this school the best!

Some of you may ask what qualities I have that make me the obvious choice for school councillor. First of all, I would make it my policy to listen to any suggestions you put forward. My role would be to represent your feelings and ideas. Surely we do not want people who refuse to listen to other people's ideas? We all know those ignorant people who never take the time to find out how other people think. Would they give you the chance to influence what goes on in the school? On the contrary, with me, if you have something to say, let me say it for you on the council.

Most of you will be aware that I am not afraid about speaking up. This may also be true of others who want your vote. The difference is, that I am able to speak up without causing offence to adults or other children. As a result, I am adept at getting others to agree to a point of view. People with any sense realise that this essential quality of mine is the most likely to succeed in getting changes made. Imagine how some of the people who are asking for your vote would behave. Some would never speak up, some would bore everyone by not being able to put their views across and some would simply be so rude, their views would not be listened to.

Moreover, although your ideas and suggestions will be an important element of my role on the council, what is also needed is a strong leader that can make fantastic changes happen. The person you elect must have brilliant ideas of their own and be strong enough to carry them through. My manifesto demonstrates the sort of new ideas that I will be putting forward to make this school the best. It is true that some of you will have your own ideas, but you will find that mine are exciting and these are just the beginnings!

These are my ideas… (Here the author lists the ideas for the school.)

Choosing the right person to represent you on the School Council is your chance to influence changes that will improve your experiences at school. Do you want to waste this chance? You should choose someone who will listen to you, speak well and who has great ideas of their own. I am the only person who fits this description. Vote for me and you will be voting for changes that don't just make things better – but make changes for the best!

Chapter 6

Discussion writing

What is a discussion text?

A discussion text presents arguments for different points of view on a topic.

Structural features

- Usually begins with an opening statement to indicate the issue that is to be discussed

- Main body of text lists the arguments for and against the point of view supported by evidence and reasoning

- Ends with a conclusion that reiterates the opening statement and presents a summary of the arguments presented

Linguistic features

- Usually present tense, third person

- Formal, impersonal style

- Use of connectives to show logic (therefore, however, because of, due to, despite, this shows, in spite of, as a result of)

Examples of discussion texts

- debates
- book reviews
- newspaper editorials
- academic essays
- leaflets/pamphlets on controversial issues

Teaching discussion writing

This genre provides children with an opportunity to understand that, although people may be passionate about their point of view, there are always two or more sides to any argument. It also gives them a chance to base their own opinions on thinking about the evidence and information available and on the opinions of others. In order to do this, the children will need to tackle many different tasks. They need to:

1. Gather information;

2. Listen to different points of view and discuss them;

3. Assess the evidence available;

4. Summarise different arguments in logical steps;

5. Maintain a balance between the arguments;

6. Make their own conclusions with reasons;

7. Use appropriate language.

It is useful to start the children off with a range of debates so that they can see the process loosely created verbally before attempting to write a discussion text. The structural and linguistic features of a discussion text should be taught explicitly to the children so that they are supported throughout the process. Using examples will enable them to understand what they are aiming towards.

Discussion writing – progression

It is not until Year 6 that children are expected to write discussion texts, but the ground work is developed in Years 4 and 5.

In Year 4 they are required to read, compare and evaluate examples of arguments and discussions (Term 3:T16,T17) and they investigate persuasive writing (Term 3:T18).

In Year 5, the children are expected to construct an argument to persuade others of a point of view and evaluate its effectiveness (Term 3:T19).

In **Year 6** the children are taught to recognise how arguments are constructed in order to be effective and to identify the features of balanced written arguments. They are expected to construct effective arguments and write balanced reports of controversial issues (Term 2:T15, T16,T18,T19). They are taught to identify the key features of impersonal formal language. They are expected to select the appropriate style and form to suit a specific audience, drawing on their knowledge of different non-fiction text types (Term 3:T16,T22).

Unit 1

Lesson focus

History Unit 14 – Who were the ancient Greeks?

Overall aim

To write a discussion text about the best place to live in ancient Greek times – Athens or Sparta.

History emphasis

In this unit the children will learn about issues surrounding education, the place and roles of females in society and the controversies surrounding intellectual prowess versus physical might. It is important for the children to realise that the judgements we make on these civilisations today are from the context of current thinking. They will need to understand that people who lived thousands of years ago were in a different situation to people today. A key skill in history is to be able to learn from the past cultures in order to rationalise choices made today.

Literacy links

Year 6, Term 2: T15, T16, T18, T19, S5

About this unit

Before the children begin this unit, they will need some knowledge of Ancient Greece. They will be investigating the two city states of Athens and Sparta and finding out the differences between the ideas and organisations of these two societies. This will require from the children an analytical skill and they can be encouraged to transfer their reasoning to current political problems. Through role play, the children will make 'typical' statements from the two city states. They will have opportunities for debate which will require logical thinking and an opportunity for enhancing speaking and listening skills.

Switching on

Learning objectives

- To begin to understand different points of view.
- To find out about the life of people living in Athens and Sparta in the time of Ancient Greece.

Resources

- Sheets B and C (pages 107 and 108)
- A map showing the location of Athens and the area where Sparta used to be

What to do

Remind the children about recent work done on Ancient Greece. Tell them that today they are going to find out about some of the different ideas people had who lived in the ancient city state of Athens and the ancient city state of Sparta.

Show the children the map, pointing out Athens and its place near the coast. Ask them if they can suggest any benefits from living near the sea (easy travel by boat to

other places, easy travel by others to Athens, trade from across the known world). Write up their ideas.

Show them where Sparta was. Ask them if they can suggest any benefits from living in this location (easy to defend, richer soil). Write up their ideas.

Ask the children if they can suggest any consequences of living in the two places. Help them consider this by asking the following questions:

If you live near the sea and are meeting people from other cultures all the time, what might be the effects on your daily life/art/music/ideas?

If you live inland, surrounded by mountains and other city states, and you hardly ever met people from other cultures, what might you fear? What might happen to your daily life/art/music/ideas?

Tell the children that they are now going to read some information about the lives of the people living in the two

places. Share an enlarged version of Sheet B. Discuss any unfamiliar terms, making sure the children have understood the content of the text.

Generate a brief, general discussion about the two places, encouraging the children to give their opinions about what it must have been like to live there at that time. For example, ask them to tell you what they think are the negative aspects about living in Athens and the negative aspects about living in Sparta. Ask them if there are any points about either place that make it a better place to live (in their opinion). It may be very useful to create a short list of the differences between the two places, for example:

	Athens	Sparta
women	stayed home	more freedom
education/ training	only for boys	boys and girls trained to be soldiers
values	intelligence, culture, the mind	strength, beauty, the body
government	could vote (but not slaves or women)	no voting

Tell them that they are going to explore these ideas further by carrying out a role play activity. Provide each child with a copy of Sheet C. Explain that the comments in the speech bubbles could come from an Athenian or a Spartan and that they are going to try and work out which comment has come from which person. Explain that the role play involves one of them being an Athenian and one of them being a Spartan. The Athenian, for example, has to choose a comment from the sheet that he or she thinks an Athenian would say and the other child has to choose a comment that he or she thinks the Spartan would say in reply. Tell them that you are going to show them how to do this. Explain that you are going to be the Athenian and that they are going to be the Spartan. Ask them to pick out a few comments that they think belong to the Spartan and put these to you. Tell them you will try to answer the point by reading a comment from the sheet that an Athenian would probably reply. For example:

Child (Spartan): Our people are the best soldiers in the world. We fight to get what we want.

You (Athenian): It's important to be able to try and solve conflicts through discussion.

Child (Spartan): A hard life is a good life.

You (Athenian): A gentle, cultured life is a good life.

Explain that you now want them to work in pairs for fifteen minutes to try this themselves. One child is to be Athenian, the other Spartan. Each child is to pick out the comments that relate to their role play character and express them orally to the other. The other has to try and reply with a counter-argument. If they use up all the comments before the end of this time, they are to generate more comments from either side.

Plenary

After fifteen minutes, gather the children together again. Go through each commentary, asking them if they think it belongs to an Athenian or a Spartan. If a child makes an inappropriate suggestion, explain why the commentary belongs to the other side. Ask them to tell you which place they would prefer to live and give their reasons why. Ask the children to provide further examples of typical comments from Athenians and Spartans.

Revving up

Learning objectives

■ To investigate the structural and linguistic features of a discussion text.

Resources

■ Sheets A and B (pages 106 and 107)

What to do

Remind the children about the text they recently shared about Athens and Sparta. Tell them that it was a discussion text and that they are going to be writing their own discussion text later about whether it would be better to live in Sparta or Athens.

Explain that a discussion text presents an argument and information from different points of view and uses particular types of words and phrases. Tell them that they are going to learn about the special features of a discussion text in order to help them write their own.

Share an enlarged version of Sheet B and reread the text. Introduce the structural features first by writing on the board a list of the following: 'introduction', 'arguments for a point of view', 'arguments against a point of view', 'summary/conclusion'.

Point to the introduction and explain that it tells the reader what the text is going to be about – it puts the arguments into a context. Explain that the introduction points out the main issues to be addressed (Athens and Sparta located differently, the effects of this location). Underline the sentence that ends 'but were they completely better than the Spartans?' Tell them that this clearly points out what the discussion is going to be about.

Tell the children that after the introduction the text is divided up into paragraphs that present the arguments for and against a point of view.

Explain that the first three paragraphs make arguments for the point of view that the Athenians weren't perfect. (They limited the role of women, the education of girls, and democracy to free men only.) Tell them that the second three paragraphs argue that the Spartans had good points. (They gave women greater freedom, they protected their way of life and improved it by war, and they were good at winning.) Explain that a discussion text should be organised so that there are equal amounts of points for each side of an argument.

Next, point to the last paragraph and ask the children to tell you what it contains. Agree that it provides a summary of the text. Explain that there is no need to repeat all the points mentioned, just an overview of the different opinions.

Tell the children that they are now going to look at the way the text is written and the types of words and phrases used. Ask them to tell you what they notice about the style that it is written in. Agree that it is a formal, impersonal style and is written in the past tense because it is about the past. Discuss the meaning of 'generic' terms and point out that words such as 'Athenians', 'children', 'women' and 'soldiers' are used rather than the names of specific people.

Write the term 'logical connectives' on the board and explain that these are words and phrases that have a 'cause and effect' influence on the text. Point out some examples, such as:

The Athenians thought that <u>if</u> you were a woman, you should have a fairly restricted life.

The Spartans, <u>on the other hand</u>, believed in much greater freedom for women.

Challenge the children to find other examples in the text.

Finally, provide them with their own copy of Sheet B. Ask them to work with a partner to label the following things on the sheet:

introduction;

past tense;

argument for Athenian point of view;

argument for Spartan point of view;

logical connective;

conclusion.

Plenary

Agree the features of the text by sharing an enlarged version of Sheet A.

Carry out a discussion about whether it is better to live in Athens or Sparta. Ask the children to provide three arguments with reasons for why they would like to live in Athens and three arguments with reasons for why they would like to live in Sparta.

Taking off

Learning objectives

■ To plan a discussion text.

■ To write an introduction.

Resources

■ Sticky notes

What to do

Tell the children that they are now going to plan their own discussion text about whether it would be better to have lived in Athens or Sparta. Explain that they are going to use sticky notes to organise their texts. Ask them to work in pairs or small groups and to think of the same amount of arguments against living in Athens as for living in Athens. Tell them to repeat this for Sparta. Ask them to agree the fors and againsts and then write each one on a separate sticky note. Tell them this will help them to plan their paragraphs in their text.

After about ten minutes, bring the class back together again to share their ideas. Explain that you are now going to show them how to write the introduction.

Explain that you are going to 'think aloud' so that they can see and hear the writing process. The following is for your eyes only that you can use or adapt as you wish. What you say is written in italics, what you write is written in bold.

I am going to write a discussion on whether it would be better to live in Athens or Sparta. First I have to tell the reader what the context is; in other words, why I am writing this discussion. I'm writing this because we are studying the differences between the two city states and trying to decide which would be a better place to live. So I shall write that.

In Class 6 we are studying the differences between the city states of Athens and Sparta in Ancient Greece and which would be a better place to live.

Now I have to give a statement about the issues. Well, what are the issues? The first issue could be that the people of Athens valued thinking about stuff like arts, architecture and an education that would prepare people for times of peace as well as war. I think that's a general overview of Athens, so I shall write it.

The people of Athens liked thinking, the arts, music, debate and building wonderful architecture. They thought that they should educate their children so that they could enjoy times of peace as well as having to live through times of war.

Now, I've got to put something about the issues concerning Sparta.

The Spartans, on the other hand, believed that everyone should always be ready for war. They thought that strict rules were necessary in a society.

I think that will do as an introduction. Let me read it back. Have I used the past tense? Have I used generic terms?

Ask the children to work in pairs to write their own introductions.

Plenary

Ask for some examples of introductions and discuss whether they tell the reader why the children are writing the discussion text. If everyone agrees, write the introduction on the board and ask them to find features of a discussion text in the writing or help the author of the work to add features.

Flying solo

Learning objectives

■ To write a discussion text.

Resources

■ Children's work from 'Taking off'

What to do

Tell the children they are going to complete their discussion texts today. Explain that you are going to show them how to use their sticky notes to help them write the main paragraphs of the text.

The following is for your eyes only that you can use or adapt as you wish. What you say is written in italics, what you write is written in bold.

Now, I have already written my introduction. What I have to do now is put about three arguments that agree with the point of view that Athens was not a good place to live. If we tell the reader what we think was wrong with each state, it will be easier for us and them to decide what could be avoided by living in the other state. So what was wrong with Athens? Let me look at my sticky notes. Well, one thing for sure was that women had no role apart from looking after the household. So I'll put that first.

If you were a woman in ancient Athens, all your life was revolved around the home. You were not expected to use your mind at all. A woman was not allowed to vote and so could not change the way the men made the rules about women's lives. A woman was only allowed out to certain things and the men made sure that, even if they went to the Agora, the women were guarded by themselves or male slaves.

Now, let me look at what I have written. I have included in my introduction the context and main issues. I have begun my arguments against Athens. I am using generic terms, like 'woman' and 'citizen' (point to these on the board). Have I got a logical connective? I have the word 'if', let me pop in 'then'. (Add 'then' after 'Athens' and before 'all'.) I could change the last sentence so that it reads 'Only if the women were guarded by their husbands or a male slave could they go to the Agora', but I may choose to leave that connective for another paragraph.

At this point, tell the children that they can help you write the next paragraph. Ask them to look at their sticky notes and choose a point they think is against living in Athens. Ask them to suggest to you how you should write it. Write their suggestion on the board, discussing and changing the words as you go, if necessary. At some point, tell the children that you need a connective (if necessary, remind them of a few examples). If they suggest a generic term, point this out to them and congratulate them.

Then ask the children to write their own paragraphs. It is important during the writing process, that children are given time to think and write – so stand back and do not interrupt the process if possible. Depending on the nature of the class, however, it may be necessary to work with a group of children and do a shared writing of a discussion text. Use their sticky notes and ask them to suggest what to put and in what order, with your guidance. Then ask the children to write up their decisions.

After about 15 minutes, bring the class together again and model how to write the conclusion. Remind them that the conclusion needs to sum up what they have said very briefly.

Plenary

Divide the class up into Athenians, Spartans and judges. Tell them that the Athenians and Spartans have ten minutes to come up with sound arguments for their way of life and after that they will have to persuade the judges to 'come and live with them'. During this ten minutes, the judges will be reading through the discussion texts and thinking about what will persuade them. Give the Athenians and the Spartans an equal amount of time to give their points of view. Then let the judges vote.

Was the Athenian way of life better than the Spartans'?

Athens is situated near the coast, so the ancient Athenians were in a situation where they could trade with people from overseas. This provided them with influences which could have made them outgoing and cosmopolitan. The Spartans lived inland and did not have so many opportunities to meet people from other cultures. They may have become inward looking and more suspicious of others. The Athenians may appear to have been more civilised, but were they completely better than the Spartans?

The Athenians thought that if you were a woman, you should have a fairly restricted life. They believed that women could attend weddings, funerals, religious festivals and visit female neighbours that lived close by, but that they should mostly stay at home.

They also believed that education should be mostly for the boys. This education, they thought, should include the arts, government and public speaking. The boys would have a slave tutor at home until they were six or seven and then attend school until they were eighteen. The Athenians thought that they should educate their citizens for times of peace as well as war and so the boys would not go into military service until they had finished school.

In Athens, it was considered important to be cultured and intellectual. In their opinion, people had a right to choose their government and so they invented democracy.

The Spartans, on the other hand, believed in much greater freedom for women. They proved this by making the men live in army barracks with other soldiers until they were sixty, so married Spartan women could do much as they pleased while their husbands were away.

Another thing the Spartans believed in was that girls should be trained in a similar way to the boys. They thought that they should train their citizens mostly for war. In order to make sure this happened, they took children away at the age of six or seven to be trained as soldiers. The Spartans felt that they should harden these children up and so they allowed older children to beat the younger ones who were not allowed to cry out.

In Sparta, what was valued was physical strength and beauty. They believed that being able to fight, be cunning and strong was the main aim in life. For them, it was not the taking part that mattered, but the winning and they wanted to win every battle, no matter what the cost.

It seems that the differences in opinion for the Athenians and the Spartans were the differences between intellectual and artistic ability on the one hand and the ability to be tough and strong on the other. It is hard to judge the opinions held by these different city states as we live in very different times. However, the Athenians could have learned something about freedom for women and the Spartans could have learned something about the good effects of valuing thought.

opening statement/ introduction

logical connective

generic term

past tense

arguments for the point of view are listed, supported by reasons

concluding statement

statement of issues is presented

para 2 argument for the Athenian point of view

para 3 & 4 argument for the Athenian point of view

para 5, 6 & 7 argument for the Spartan point of view

Was the Athenian way of life better than the Spartans'?

Athens is situated near the coast, so the ancient Athenians were in a situation where they could trade with people from overseas. This provided them with influences which could have made them outgoing and cosmopolitan. The Spartans lived inland and did not have so many opportunities to meet people from other cultures. They may have become inward looking and more suspicious of others. The Athenians may appear to have been more civilised, but were they completely better than the Spartans?

The Athenians thought that if you were a woman, you should have a fairly restricted life. They believed that women could attend weddings, funerals, religious festivals and visit female neighbours that lived close by, but that they should mostly stay at home.

They also believed that education should be mostly for the boys. This education, they thought, should include the arts, government and public speaking. The boys would have a slave tutor at home until they were six or seven and then attend school until they were eighteen. The Athenians thought that they should educate their citizens for times of peace as well as war and so the boys would not go into military service until they had finished school.

In Athens, it was considered important to be cultured and intellectual. In their opinion, people had a right to choose their government and so they invented democracy.

The Spartans, on the other hand, believed in much greater freedom for women. They proved this by making the men live in army barracks with other soldiers until they were sixty, so married Spartan women could do much as they pleased while their husbands were away.

Another thing the Spartans believed in was that girls should be trained in a similar way to the boys. They thought that they should train their citizens mostly for war. In order to make sure this happened, they took children away at the age of six or seven to be trained as soldiers. The Spartans felt that they should harden these children up and so they allowed older children to beat the younger ones who were not allowed to cry out.

In Sparta, what was valued was physical strength and beauty. They believed that being able to fight, be cunning and strong was the main aim in life. For them, it was not the taking part that mattered, but the winning and they wanted to win every battle, no matter what the cost.

It seems that the differences in opinion for the Athenians and the Spartans were the differences between intellectual and artistic ability on the one hand and the ability to be tough and strong on the other. It is hard to judge the opinions held by these different city states as we live in very different times. However, the Athenians could have learned something about freedom for women and the Spartans could have learned something about the good effects of valuing thought.

Writing across the Curriculum

> Eating little, hard physical exercise, bare living quarters and a tough outlook on life – that's what's needed.

> You're savages – you don't even let your people vote!

> A hard life is a good life.

> Women are only good to look after children.

> We like to meet and learn from other people.

> Music, art, literature, crafts, ideas, architecture and democracy – that's what's needed.

> Our people are the best soldiers in the world. We fight to get what we want.

> The mind is important – it's what separates us from the beasts.

> Rules are what you need. You need a government that tells the people what to do.

> The body is the most important thing. Our people are fit and strong.

> We like to meet and learn from other people.

> A gentle, cultured life is a good life.

> It's important to be able to solve conflicts through discussion.

> Who needs other people? They will try to take you over unless you can protect yourself.

Unit 2

Lesson focus

Geography Unit 16 – What's in the news?

Overall aim

To write a discussion text about the environmental issues surrounding a proposed bypass.

Geography emphasis

The lessons in this unit focus on recent or proposed changes in a locality and how these changes affect the environment. A geographical skill that will be developed is an awareness of the diversity of people that are affected when changes in a locality occur. It also requires children to understand that a locality usually contains a variety of environments and that balancing the needs of these environments with the needs of people is a challenging task. As our landscape becomes ever more urbanised, today's children will undoubtedly be faced with these problems at sometime and therefore need to be made aware of the issues concerned.

Literacy links

Year 6, Term 2: T15, T16, T18, T19, S5

About this unit

A variety of different opinions on a single issue will be presented to the children and this will require them to sift through information and opinions in order to make their own. They will need to be able to see things from different perspectives and make reasoned conclusions. The children will be encouraged to make balanced arguments for and against a proposal. Through debate, they will reinforce the skills of concentration, formulating their opinions into coherent and structured speech which will build on other children's points of view.

Switching on

Learning objectives

■ To gather information and understand the issues.

■ To formulate own opinions.

■ To contribute to group discussions.

Resources

■ Sheet A (page 114)

■ Sheet B (pages 115 and 116) cut up into separate letters to the editor

What to do

Tell the children you are going to read a newspaper report to them about a proposed bypass. Read out an enlarged version of Sheet A. Ask them if they can think of any environmental problems with the proposed plan. Write their ideas up on the board.

Explain that people often write to the newspaper's editor in response to reports such as this one. Tell them that

they are now going to read some of these people's responses to find out what the people of Larkham think about the proposal. Explain that you want them to work in groups so that each group has a different letter each.

Divide the class into seven mixed ability groups and provide each group with one letter from Sheet B. Tell the children that you want them to read the letter and pretend that they support the views contained in it, (even if they disagree with the ideas themselves) in order to carry out a role play later. Tell them that you want them to help each other to think of lots of reasons why they could support the views in their letter. (As they have no choice but to find arguments and reasons for the particular point of view, they are encouraged to be objective in their thinking. This also provides for the children the challenge of seeing things from an alternative point of view. Later on, they will be making their own decisions, based on information and listening to other people's points of view.)

After they have had time to read the letter and share their ideas, ask each group to read their letter to the rest of the class. Write up on the board who the letter represents:

Edward Banks – farmer

Mrs May Jones – elderly resident

Cathy Lumas – mother of young children

Sam Linton – conservationist

Mary Langley – naturalist

Dr S Poste – scientist

Sam Pepper – unemployed youth

Initiate a discussion by asking each group in turn to put forward their point of view to the rest of the class in their own words, adding anything they can think of to further their arguments and win the 'debate'. It would be useful for you to act as 'devil's advocate'. For example, if the 'farmers' say that buying food in from abroad gives them too much competition in the supermarkets, you could say, *'Yes, that's a good point, you have to agree that a glut of food from abroad pushed the prices down and farmers in this country can't produce enough food to make it cheap, so they go out of business.'* If another group point out that farmers still have 75 per cent of the land, you can turn to the farmers and say, *'Now, come on farmers, what are you moaning about?'* and so on.

After the discussion send the children off to their groups again and ask them to note down any further arguments they could generate either in support of their own group or against any of the other groups. (This is a good opportunity to assess children's speaking and listening skills.)

Plenary

Ask each group, in turn, to represent their case to the rest of the class. Allow those listening the opportunity to ask questions and encourage them to debate the issues.

Summarise the arguments under two headings – 'For' and 'Against' the new bypass. Write it on a flipchart so that the children can refer to it later.

Revving up

Learning objectives

■ To investigate the key features of a discussion text.

■ To sort and classify information.

Resources

■ Sheets A, B, C and D (pages 114–118)

■ List of 'For' and 'Against' from 'Switching on'

What to do

Remind the children about the newspaper report and letters to the editor they read in the previous lesson. Tell them that they are now going to read a discussion text about the proposed bypass. Explain that a discussion text is a written, reasoned argument giving different points of view. Tell them that they are going to find out about the special features of a discussion text in order to help them write their own discussion later on.

Share an enlarged version of Sheet D. Discuss any unfamiliar terms and make sure the children understand the content of the text by asking relevant questions such as:

Why are the farmers worried about the bypass?

What is so special about Curlew Marsh?

Who dislikes traffic coming through the town?

Explain the structural features of the text first, using Sheet C as your guide: an opening statement, paragraphs with arguments for and against a point of view and a conclusion. Annotate these features on the enlarged version. Point out that each part of the structure has its own paragraph and that there are as many arguments for a point of view as there are against, which makes the discussion balanced.

Next, discuss the linguistic features. Point out that it is written in the present tense (for example, 'Residents in Larkham claim'). Point out that personal pronouns, such as 'she', 'he', 'his' and so on are not usually used, but generic terms such as 'residents', 'elderly people' and 'conservationists' are used instead. Ask them to give you further examples from the text – you could underline them.

Show the children examples of conditional connectives. Write on the board a list of conditional connectives (If … then, might, could, unless, providing, only if, even if, on condition). Spend a few minutes discussing how these can be used.

Remind the children that they are going to use these features to write their own discussion texts in the next lesson, but first they need to gather and sort the evidence. Tell them to work in pairs and to prepare two pieces of paper, one headed 'For' and the other headed 'Against'. Tell them to gather as many arguments as possible and to write these on to the appropriate piece of paper. It would be helpful to keep on display the enlarged version of Sheet D as well as Sheets A and B. Walk around the class and assist where necessary.

Plenary

When they have finished, ask them if they have any of their own ideas to add to the arguments or evidence that they can share with the class. Ask them to make sure they have enough arguments and evidence to create a 'balanced' discussion text.

Taking off

Learning objectives

■ To plan a discussion text.
■ To use linguistic features of a discussion text.

Resources

■ Sheet E (page 119)
■ Children's work from 'Revving up'

What to do

Tell the children that they are now going to plan their own discussion text about the proposed bypass. Explain that to help them, you are going to show them how to use a writing frame to do the planning. Show an enlarged version of Sheet E. As you write, think aloud so that the children can hear and see the process. Below is a script for your eyes only which you can use or adapt as you wish. What you say is in italics, what you write is in bold.

Now, what is the first thing I must do? I must say what we are discussing and tell the reader the main arguments or issues.

In class … we are discussing whether or not a bypass to the small market town of Larkham is a good idea.

What are the main issues? Let me think.

The people who live in the town are fed up with the increase of traffic through their high street, but others think a bypass will cause environmental damage to the surrounding countryside.

Let me look at what I have just written. I have made a statement about what we are doing and the main arguments, but have I used the simple present tense? Yes, look, 'who live in the town'. Have I used a generic term for people? Yes, I have said 'people', not Mrs Jones or Bob the builder! Have I used a conditional conjunction? No. Let me put one in.(Wipe out 'will' and put in 'might'.)

What is the next step? If we look at Sheet E, the first three boxes want the arguments for one side of the debate. I will put my first argument for the bypass in the box that says 'Some people think that...'

Now involve the children. Ask them to give you an argument for the bypass to put in this box. Tell them they can share with the writing. Write an argument and ask the children to correct it if necessary, emphasising the use of generic terms and conditional conjunctions. Go through the headings, suggesting what may be put in each box.

When you feel the children understand what they need to do, provide them with their own copies of Sheet E and ask them to plan their own work.

Plenary

Gather the children together and ask some of them to read out their plans. Ensure balanced arguments and concise language. If there is a child who has had difficulty writing a conclusion, ask the child if you could use it to help the others in the class by a shared writing plenary.

Flying solo

Learning objectives

■ To write a discussion text.

Resources

■ Children's work from 'Taking off'
■ 'For' and 'against' lists

What to do

Tell the children that they are now going to use their planning sheets to write their own discussion text. Ask them to remind you about the structure of a discussion text.

Briefly revise the linguistic features they should be using, for example, ask them if it is right to say 'Mrs Black thinks' or 'Farmer Giles says'. Discuss generic terms. Remind them about the use of the simple present tense by writing the following sentences on the board and asking them which one would be the correct tense for a discussion text:

Elderly residents were upset because the heavy traffic made so much noise.

Elderly residents are upset because the heavy traffic makes so much noise.

Elderly residents will be upset because the heavy traffic will make so much noise.

Ask them if they have any questions or problems with writing their discussion texts and then set them off to write their own.

It is important to give the children an opportunity to work on their own so others, including the teacher, do not interrupt them. Although you should 'stand back' at this point, a particular group may need support or enrichment. If working with a group that needs support, sit with the children and work together on building their discussion texts, pointing out the structure and suggesting generic terms and conditional conjunctions. If a group needs enrichment, allow them some time to write and then ask them to share the writing with you and others in the group. Share good points and ask for suggestions on how the writing could be improved. Allow the children time to redraft/correct/think about any improvements they wish to make.

Plenary

At the end of the session, tell the children that many people find writing a discussion text very difficult, even at university, so they have done very well.

Tell them that they can now have a debate on the issues using their own points of view. Manage the debate by asking those who would be 'for' the bypass to sit on one side of the room and those 'against' to sit on the other. This is a good opportunity to encourage sound speaking and listening skills. Act as chairperson and encourage the children to think before they speak, raise hands before speaking and demonstrate good listening skills by referring to a point made by the other side and building on it.

The Larkham Post
Wednesday, 13th October 2004

PLANS FOR NEW LARKHAM BYPASS

The Larkham Town Council is considering approving plans for a new bypass that will link the A27 from Eastbourne to the M23 north of Crawley. The proposed route will run alongside the River Ouse and cut through Curlew Marsh on the west side of Larkham.

Town councillor, Mr Benjamin Watts, said today "Larkham has become one of the fastest growing small towns in the South East of England. It is on a direct line between the South Coast and London. In spite of good railway connections, the amount of through traffic in its narrow lanes has become insupportable. The roads in Larkham were not built to accommodate the current level of traffic. Larkham has become noisy, dangerous and polluted. The proposed new bypass will provide easy access to London and the South Coast for all the residents of Larkham and the surrounding area. It will also return Larkham itself to

a delightful and peaceful area to live."

If the new bypass goes ahead, the large supermarket chain 'Findles' will apply for planning permission to build a hypermarket in the area between Larkham and the new bypass. This will be using land that is currently farmland.

Our editor, Sally Green, would welcome views from our readers.

Madam

If Findles build the hypermarket in the suggested area, it will be my farmland that is affected. Your readers may not realise that every kilometre of bypass will use up three hectares of good arable land. Seventy five per cent of land in the UK is farmland, but we are still importing vast quantities of food from abroad. By losing farmland we are further reducing our ability to feed ourselves as a nation. Although no doubt I would be well compensated for the loss of my farmland, people should think about the effects on the landscape, the crops we grow and the animals this land supports. Our lives as farmers are in increasing peril from the growth of buildings and motorways in this country.

Edward Banks, Farmer

Dear Miss Editor

I have lived in Larkham for all of my 75 years. It has grown from a sleepy village to a bustling town. As I live in one of the cottages on the main road through Larkham, I can tell you that the terrible noise from the cars and lorries passing all day and night has ruined what could be my final days. The air is awful with exhaust fumes and I suffer from asthma and bronchitis. Anything that returns Larkham to a place where I can live without being ill would be very welcome.

Mrs May Jones

Madam Editor

As your readers know, the River Ouse that passes just two miles from Larkham centre, is an area of outstanding natural beauty. Most use this area for a wide variety of recreational purposes such as walking, cycling and canoeing. It is also a natural habitat for all sorts of wildlife. This proposed route for the bypass will destroy the ecosystem of this part of the river. You will lose the plants that feed the insects and herbivores such as rabbits, mice and voles, which in turn means losing the carnivores such as foxes, weasels and kestrels. It is too high a price to pay for a quieter road through Larkham.

Sam Linton, Larkham River Ouse Conservation Society

Dear Sally

As a parent with three small children, I would like to point out that the levels of lead pollution from exhaust fumes in Larkham can be very dangerous. Lead enters the body and once it is there it stays there. If these levels are not reduced, brain damage can occur. Children are particularly vulnerable.

Cathy Lumas

My Dear Ms Green

Curlew Marsh is of special scientific interest. It contains a number of rare species of plants that support rare insects. If the bypass cuts through this area, these will be lost to us and our children forever.

Mary Langley, Naturalist

Madam

I have researched the effects of new motorways in other areas and I have produced for the benefit of your readers a chart showing the effects of people on the environment over the centuries. You will see that, although the new bypass may affect local habitats and ecosystems temporarily, the grass verges by the side of motorways create a new habitat for wild life.

Dr S. Poste
Geographical Research Unit
Camberway University

Dear Sally

Has anyone considered the amount of jobs that would be created by the bypass? Apart from work on the bypass and its upkeep, the supermarket would create many jobs for those of us who are unemployed. Many of us young people will have to move away to find work unless this bypass is built. What would happen to Larkham without its young people?

Sam Pepper

opening statement/ introduction

statement of issues is presented

The Larkham Bypass

Larkham, a small market town in the South of England, has seen a heavy increase in through traffic over recent years, which causes environmental hazards to the residents of Larkham. However, the bypass will be a major road that will cut through local countryside and farmland and it would affect a range of important local habitats.

logical connective

para 2 arguments for with evidence

Residents in Larkham claim that if the amount of lead in the atmosphere, caused by the exhaust fumes from the heavy traffic, increases, then their health will be badly affected. They are particularly concerned for the children as, once lead enters the blood stream it cannot be removed and can cause brain damage. Providing the bypass is constructed, the air in Larkham will improve and become healthier.

present tense

para 3 & 4 arguments for with evidence

Elderly people are also keen on the construction of the bypass. They feel that the amount of noise made by the traffic in the main road and the potential hazards of crossing this busy road, has made their lives miserable. Many of these elderly people have lived in Larkham all their lives and are very upset by the recent changes. They want to see Larkham returning to the peaceful small town it used to be.

generic term

Scientific researchers claim that the new bypass will only affect the local habitats in the short term. They have found that, after many years, new habitats form along the sides of motorways.

para 4, 5 & 6 arguments against with evidence

However, there are many people who think that the new bypass will create more problems than it solves. Local farmers are particularly worried about the loss of farmland. They say that England is fast losing its ability to grow its own food and already imports vast quantities from abroad. They are also concerned because the farmland supports many habitats. Only by looking after these habitats, such as hedgerows, will these ecosystems survive.

Conservationists are also worried about the proposed route as it will go alongside the River Ouse for several miles and cross it at a certain point. This will not only spoil the River Ouse as a recreational area for local people, but will destroy the ecosystem along this part of the river. This in turn, they say, could affect the ecosystem for long stretches of the river in both directions. In particular, the conservationists say that animals such as foxes, weasels and kestrels will disappear.

Naturalists point out that if the new bypass cuts through Curlew Marsh, many rare species of plants and insects will be lost to future generations.

summary

On the one hand, it seems that people living in the town of Larkham have their lives put at risk or are at least put under enormous strain by the heavy loads of traffic passing through the town. A new bypass will improve their daily living conditions. On the other hand, the proposed route will destroy many important habitats, at least in the short term. It would also badly affect the already struggling farming community.

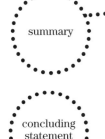

concluding statement

Perhaps a solution may be in trying to look at different routes for the new bypass or encouraging the traffic to use other means of transport by making the good railway links more attractive and reliable.

The Larkham Bypass

Larkham, a small market town in the South of England, has seen a heavy increase in through traffic over recent years, which causes environmental hazards to the residents of Larkham. However, the bypass will be a major road that will cut through local countryside and farmland and it would affect a range of important local habitats.

Residents in Larkham claim that if the amount of lead in the atmosphere, caused by the exhaust fumes from the heavy traffic, increases, then their health will be badly affected. They are particularly concerned for the children as, once lead enters the blood stream it cannot be removed and can cause brain damage. Providing the bypass is constructed, the air in Larkham will improve and become healthier.

Elderly people are also keen on the construction of the bypass. They feel that the amount of noise made by the traffic in the main road and the potential hazards of crossing this busy road, has made their lives miserable. Many of these elderly people have lived in Larkham all their lives and are very upset by the recent changes. They want to see Larkham returning to the peaceful small town it used to be.

Scientific researchers claim that the new bypass will only affect the local habitats in the short term. They have found that, after many years, new habitats form along the sides of motorways.

However, there are many people who think that the new bypass will create more problems than it solves. Local farmers are particularly worried about the loss of farmland. They say that England is fast losing its ability to grow its own food and already imports vast quantities from abroad. They are also concerned because the farmland supports many habitats. Only by looking after these habitats, such as hedgerows, will these ecosystems survive.

Conservationists are also worried about the proposed route as it will go alongside the River Ouse for several miles and cross it at a certain point. This will not only spoil the River Ouse as a recreational area for local people, but will destroy the ecosystem along this part of the river. This in turn, they say, could affect the ecosystem for long stretches of the river in both directions. In particular, the conservationists say that animals such as foxes, weasels and kestrels will disappear.

Naturalists point out that if the new bypass cuts through Curlew Marsh, many rare species of plants and insects will be lost to future generations.

On the one hand, it seems that people living in the town of Larkham have their lives put at risk or are at least put under enormous strain by the heavy loads of traffic passing through the town. A new bypass will improve their daily living conditions. On the other hand, the proposed route will destroy many important habitats, at least in the short term. It would also badly affect the already struggling farming community.

Perhaps a solution may be in trying to look at different routes for the new bypass or encouraging the traffic to use other means of transport by making the good railway links more attractive and reliable.

In class _____we are discussing whether

Some people think that

because

Others, such as _____agree,
because

Another point raised by _____ is

However, _____ think that

Also,

_____ says that

To sum up the different points of view, I would say that

I think

because